SCHOLASTIC

Brain-Based
Strategies to Reach Every Learner

Surveys, Questionnaires, and Checklists That Help You Identify Student's Strengths—Plus Brain-Based Lessons and Activities for Engaging Every Learner

J. Diane Connell, Ed.D.

New York • Toronto • London • Auckland • Sydney
Mexico City • New Delhi • Hong Kong • Buenos Aires

Teaching Resources

Cover design by Adana Jimenez
Interior design by Sarah Morrow
Illustrations on pages 67–68 by Kathie Kelleher

Published by Scholastic Inc.
Printed in the U.S.A.
ISBN 0-439-59020-5

3 4 5 6 7 8 9 10 40 11 10 09 08 07 06

Dedication

This book is dedicated to the three splendid "young" men in my life: my loving husband, Jim, for 21 spectacular years of marriage, and to my two magnificent sons, Jason, 19, and Robert, 16. Your lives are an absolute privilege and joy to share! It has been an honor to connect with all of you, and to share our amazing, developing lives as a family. Jason and Robert, I am extraordinarily proud of the young men that you have developed into; Jim, thank you for your strength, support, understanding, and willingness to let both of us grow and change as our time together marches on.

This book is also dedicated to *two absolutely Spectacularly Wonderful women*, Janie and Betsy, who continually support me with Guidance, Enlightenment, and Love. It is an absolute privilege to be part of your awe-inspiring network. (1) To Janie Faye Osborne Sastre, for over 30 years you have been my Sister of the Spirit and of the Universe; you are my Sister in Adventure, Travel, Compassion, and Teaching. Thank you for our weekly IM's, Ma and Pa, for always listening, clarifying, and encouraging me; for sharing yourself with me; and for repeatedly telling me, in clever words and heart-felt messages that "you *can* do this; I'm with you; you did it! Yay!" Janie, our travels have just begun! (2) To Betsy Gunzelmann, for over 16 years, you have been my Sister spanning connections in both our Personal and our Professional Worlds. Thank you for your continual guidance on daily matters of the heart and the mind. Thank you for trusting me, for sharing yourself, for your compassion and understanding, for your amazing ability to reassure, and for your right-brained "Knowing" and splendid ability to comfort. Onward and upward we go!

And also to my Mentor and friend, Mrs. Dorothy Patton, for her help, love, and Life-Long Support; for her understanding, and for her gentle, yet firm guidance of me during the past 36 years of my life! Thank you, Dot, for shaping me into the teacher, and the person I am today. Thank you for so completely changing the course of my life.

Thank-yous go to:

. . . Julie Mundt, Bess Arnold, Diane Daniels, and Diana Kowalik, my Gentle Sisters of the Spirit, and incredibly supportive friends. Thank you for your continual spiritual guidance!

. . . Mary Raddock, whose energy, foresight, caring, voice, and abilities to analyze, support, and encourage are astounding; and for sharing Frank E. Lee, James, and Kate. Mary, you have been my Friend for 30 years—here's to the next 30 of sharing and caring!

. . . Cathy Zwolinski, for her natural abilities to share and to give of herself; and for her ability to excite the minds of her students and her friends. Thank you and your family, Mike, Michael, and Dave, for all of our very special memories.

. . . Vera Kroms, whom I have known for 28 years; for her enormous talent to soothe and to understand; for her love of nature, cats, books, poetry, and pottery; and her willingness to always help with kitties, my African violets and newspaper editorials, and for sharing Tom.

. . . Tim Mckenzie, a dear and cherished friend and colleague, and his wife Mary. Thank you Tim, for your warmth, humor and constant support; and for introducing Jim and me so many years ago.

. . . *my many wonderful friends, colleagues, administrators, staff, and students at Rivier College!*

. . . my other friends who are so gifted and talented, and so generous at "being there" for me, and who are so competent in what they do: Mindy Booth—special needs teacher and my walking buddy, and Gary, Anne, and Lisa; Lynne Rothstein—therapist and fellow sojourner from Nashville, Tennessee, and Jay, Max, and Allie; Elaine Francis—professor, and Jerry, Tim, and John; Diane Ryding—teacher, accountant, graceful hostess, and Cliff; and Kris Reilly—teacher, editor, support person.

. . . the Connell Family: Barbara Jeannie Spolidoro, Jack and Anne Marie Connell, Mary and Jay Gaudette, David and Mary Connell, Dottie, Tom, Donna, and Barbara McDermott, and our 10 wonderful nieces and nephews.

Finally, in loving memory of Lucy Connell, and my parents, Dorothy and Marvin Jacobs; and to my brother David Jacobs, and his wonderful family—Sheri, Kayla, and Bennett.

Thank you, everyone.

Gratefully,

Table of Contents

Preface

I was 17 years old when my teaching career began. My mom had taken me to the home of Dot Patton, in Nashville, Tennessee, for a course in speed-reading. Over the next four decades, Dot became my teacher, my mentor, and much later in my life, my colleague. As a junior in high school, I was surprised when she asked if I wanted to tutor adolescents who had dropped out of the Nashville school system. I saw that these "troubled" boys wanted to learn to read, and that they were happy that someone cared enough to help them.

Because of this, and other early teaching opportunities, I completed my undergraduate education with teaching certifications in elementary education, learning disabilities, and behavior disorders. I went on to earn a master's degree in educational psychology. I taught junior high and high school students before obtaining my doctorate in education from Boston University. Through the years, I have taught at different levels in the K–12 and college systems.

Currently, as an education professor at Rivier College in Nashua, New Hampshire, I primarily teach graduate students, mostly elementary teachers, who wish to obtain their master's degree in learning disabilities. But I cannot stay away from the K–12 spectrum—in the past few years I have gone into third-, fourth-, and fifth-grade classrooms in Westford, Massachusetts, to teach aspects of my Brain-Based Learning units. Components of these lessons and units have been published in *Classroom Leadership* and *Instructor.*

Over the past 15 years, I have studied and reflected upon "teaching as an art," and wondered about the biological explanations for why so many of us teach in such radically different ways. And I have looked for the most effective techniques that teachers can use to reach students with different learning needs. I have found some brain-based learning techniques that will encourage our students to *want* to learn as well as realize that they *can* learn. It is these that I share with you in this book.

I wrote this book because I know that as teachers, we are always searching for ways to enhance our teaching. Many of us now teach both regular-education students and students with special needs. I believe that you will find these strategies helpful in working with all of your students. I hope that you find this book on brain-based learning, with its neurobiological underpinnings, to be informative and invigorating.

A bibliography packed with books, articles, and Web sites is included for those who wish to further explore any of the brain-based learning ideas.

I would love to hear about your results from taking the teacher questionnaires; and the results you have had from using the brain-based methods with your students. The easiest way to contact me is by using my e-mail address printed below.

J. Diane (Jacobs) Connell, Ed.D.
Professor of Education
Rivier College
420 Main St.
Nashua, NH 03060
dconnell@rivier.edu

Chapter 1

Teacher as Learner

How We Learn Affects How We Teach

"As educators, we see every day that the process of teaching and learning requires a connection between teacher and learner. This connective process, although interpersonal, is also neurobiological."

—Mariale Hardiman (2003, p.10)

Reading this book will change your brain, and your teaching. Learning the content will help you make more neural connections in your own brain, as well as provide you with many new brain-based learning strategies to use with your students.

The goal of this book is to demonstrate how to use current knowledge of brain functioning to understand your own brain-based strengths, to enhance your teaching, and to better support your students' learning.

Teaching is both an art and a science. Learning involves change, biology, and the brain. In recent years, scientists from diverse fields—including cognitive neuroscience, biology, and psychology—have been studying how the brain functions, and how human beings learn. These scientists have found that as we learn new information, our brain actually undergoes physiological changes. These exciting discoveries about how the brain learns can be studied in conjunction with the very best ways for us to reach our students.

Teaching and learning are all about making connections. For example, psychologist Howard Gardner has identified eight kinds of intelligence, each of which has a specific location in the brain. He's found that we all have different combinations of strengths and weaknesses among these various intelligences. The implications for the classroom are staggering. Our students will learn more when teachers understand, connect with, and teach to their strengths during at least part of each day.

We can also use the findings from brain research to help our students understand their individual learning profiles. We can encourage them to work on their weaknesses, but simultaneously use their strengths to shine.

In my research, I have found that most teachers tend to rely heavily on their strengths when teaching. Awareness of your own brain preferences can help you identify areas in your teaching style that you can stretch and develop further. By expanding your teaching repertoire, you are more likely to reach a wider range of students to the benefit of everyone.

Biologist and researcher James Zull (2002) has said that "teaching is the art of changing the brain" (p. 5). Every day more and more teachers are realizing the power of this art; they are using science to understand the benefits of knowing how the brain learns. For me, the journey began when I realized that the way I teach determines whether my students will listen to me or simply tune me out. Before I was really able to connect with my students, I had to learn to thoroughly understand and accept my own, unique learning style. The theories and teaching applications gleaned from my investigations into brain-based learning helped me recognize my own strengths and weaknesses and how they affected my teaching. Once I saw the relationship of my learning style to my teaching, I was able to amend the teaching techniques that I had used habitually, and contentedly, for decades.

Discovering the Relationship Between Teaching and the Brain

In 1984, as a college professor, I began to think about the importance of understanding myself as a teacher in the classroom. Motivated initially by varying student reactions to my classes on our end-of-semester evaluations, I began to contemplate why it was that some students thought my teaching was "outstanding" while others perceived it as "average." Why did some of my students respond to me enthusiastically, while others did not? What were my teaching strengths, and my weaknesses?

Fortunately, around this same time, I read Gardner's book *Frames of Mind: The Theory of Multiple Intelligences* (1983), and I began to link two distinct concepts in my mind: the notion of what it means that I have at least eight distinct intelligences and the notion of what it means to be an effective teacher.

I soon took a multiple intelligence questionnaire, similar to the one that you can take in Chapter Five, titled "What Are My Multiple Intelligences?" From this I found out that I was *strongly developed* in Gardner's linguistic, existential, and intrapersonal intelligences; *moderately developed* in the logical-mathematical, interpersonal, musical, and naturalistic intelligences, and *underdeveloped* in the bodily-kinesthetic and spatial intelligences. Neurologically speaking, my natural learning style was one of reflection, thinking, and speaking.

I started to think about these intelligences in relation to my teaching and realized that I was primarily teaching by leaning on my strengths throughout the day. Upon further reflection, I could see that, unconsciously, I was actually avoiding the use of my underdeveloped spatial and bodily-kinesthetic intelligences.

During the next five years, to help me determine my own strengths and weaknesses, I took many brain-based learning questionnaires, including multiple intelligence scales, left brain/right brain scales, some information processing scales, as well as some emotional intelligence scales.

Slowly, patterns emerged that provided insight as to why I could challenge and motivate some of my college students, but not all of them. From the left brain/right brain literature (which I'll discuss in Chapter Four) and the Alert Scale, I concluded that I am a left-brain learner and a left-brain teacher. Essentially, this means that my left hemisphere is stronger than my right. I began to think of ways to change my teaching to compensate for this imbalance in order to reach more of my students whose learning styles were different from mine.

I now had an answer to my original question—Why did some students think my teaching was "outstanding" while others perceived it as "average"? I strongly suspect that my left-brain, linguistic students thought I was outstanding; some middle-brain students (those with neither left-brain nor right-brain dominance) were able to appreciate my lectures and discussions; but my right-brain students were bored in class with my reliance on lectures, class discussions, and research paper assignments.

My combination of strengths and weaknesses translated into a teaching style that favored numerous lectures based on research and personal teaching experiences, stimulating discussions, and lengthy, research-based assignments. It occurred to me that if I added some right-brained teaching techniques and activities, I could reach more of my students. I might reach even more if I added some different multiple-intelligence-oriented activities (specifically emphasizing my moderate and weakest areas) for my students whose learning styles were different from mine.

I was truly reluctant to cut back my well-researched lectures. Initially, I found that it did not feel either comfortable or natural to teach students using methods and activities that emphasized my weaker intelligences and the right side of the brain. With great hesitation, I started to add group work once or twice a semester. I incorporated overheads and a few humorous cartoons. I found some relevant films for my right-brained, visual/spatial learners. Although this proved challenging at first, I found that I was reaching more and more students, as my course ratings soon made clear.

Three years ago, at Rivier College in Nashua, New Hampshire, I tried using role-playing, a teaching strategy that was new and unusual for me. I designed a lesson where my undergraduate students were asked to role-play different ways that teachers could help students with special needs in the regular classroom. For example, in one situation, a second-grade teacher has a blind student transfer into her classroom. My undergraduate students role-played ways to help this special-needs student feel accepted and respected, as well as ways to help their regular second-grade students understand the disability. The entire class loved the role-playing. The middle- and right-brain learners were especially excited by a new activity that really spoke to their strengths.

As I made progress with my teaching, I wanted to share my newly found insights with my students. Since I primarily teach those whose professional goals are to become regular and/or special education teachers, it occurred to me that my students, too, would benefit from becoming aware of their own preferences, strengths, and weaknesses.

To help teachers on their own brain-based learning path, I designed and implemented a comprehensive brain-based learning plan titled "Who Am I?" This unit forms the basis of the graduate Cognition and Learning class that I coteach with Dr. Christy Hammer. Christy has said that completing the "Who Am I?" unit is like getting a brain scan without having to pay for it.

Brain-Based Strategies to Reach Every Learner is designed to offer you much the same experience as taking a graduate course in cognition and learning. Like many graduate courses, this book contains both theory and practical applications. Throughout much of the book, however, the emphasis is on you—you as a learner and as a teacher.

Who Am I? Discovering How You Learn ... and How You Teach

Teaching is a journey that does not end. One major reason that I have chosen to remain in the field for more than 30 years is that teaching allows, and encourages, us to grow and develop more fully as a person. We grow through reading new information that can be applied to our teaching, through developing new teaching techniques, through creating new lessons, and through discovering new ways to connect with our students. The evolving nature of teaching is described in the five-step teaching spiral shown below. The steps are outlined on pages 14–15. At the beginning of each chapter in this book, the steps you will be using are highlighted.

The Spiral "Who Am I?" Path

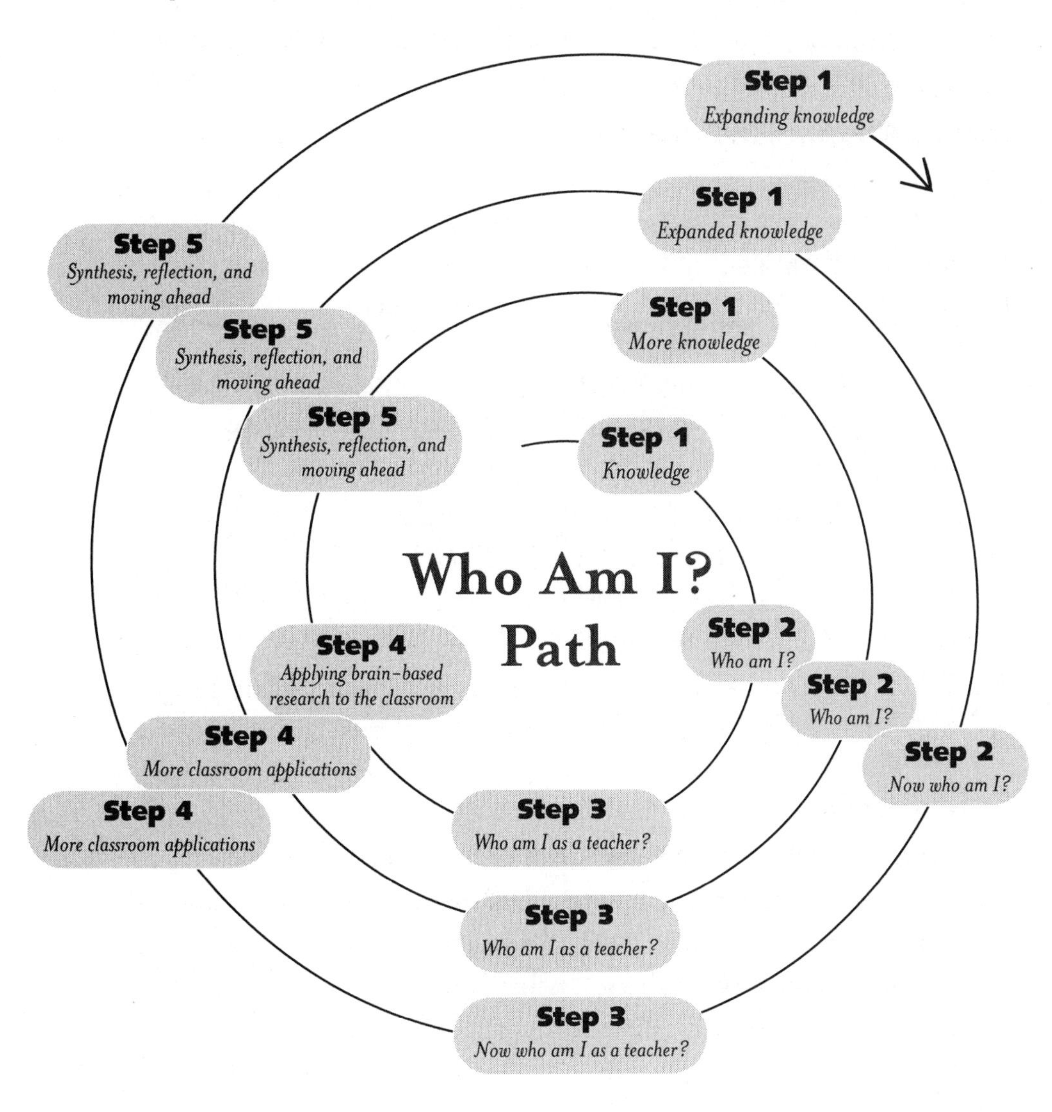

Five Steps on the Brain-Based Teaching Spiral Path

Step 1: What is brain-based learning?

The path begins as you acquire a foundation of knowledge based on the neurological, emotional, and environmental aspects of brain-based learning. Chapter Two examines the research in light of the latest developments from biology and neurology. Chapter Three covers essential brain-based learning concepts from an environmental perspective.

Step 2: Who am I, neurologically speaking?

You will see your neurological profile as measured by questionnaires found in Chapters Four, Five, Seven, and Eight. Are you a left-, right-, or middle-brain person? What are your strongest intelligences? What constitutes your strongest emotional intelligences? How do you receive, process, and express information? Information gleaned from these questionnaires will help you ascertain your own unique cognitive learning style.

Step 3: Who am I as a teacher?

Your neurological strengths guide the way you teach and the way you interact with others. In step three, you'll see how understanding your neurological proclivities will affect your teaching in positive ways.

Step 4: How can I apply brain-based research in my classroom?

Teachers primarily teach according to their neurological strengths (Connell, 2000), and we are typically adept at using our stronger intelligences in our teaching. In this step, you will be asked to expand upon your current teaching techniques by designing new lessons that use your weaker intelligences and your less dominant hemisphere. For example, in this step, you will be asked to:

- design a lesson using a left- or right-brain technique that you have not used before.
- design a lesson using one of your moderate or underdeveloped multiple intelligences.
- design a lesson using your least dominant learning style.
- design a lesson using one underdeveloped emotional domain.
- use the children's questionnaires found in Chapters Four, Five, and Seven with your students in order to enhance your understanding of their strengths and weaknesses.

Step 5: How do I continue?

The spiral does not end if our brain-based learning continues. As you read more brain-based research and create new brain-based lessons, your learning—and the steps in the spiral—will progress constantly. You will be finding new ways to teach and support all of your students, even those that are the hardest to reach.

Looking Ahead

In the next two chapters I'll give you an overview of some of the latest and most exciting brain research on how the brain works and how we learn. Chapter Two examines the research on brain physiology and its relation to learning and teaching. Chapter Three offers a discussion of Abraham Maslow's Hierarchy of Needs, and uses it to examine ways we can change our classroom environment to encourage our students to learn to their fullest potential.

Chapter 2

Brain-Based Learning

What Exactly Is Brain-Based Learning?

"Teaching is the art of changing the brain."

—James Zull (2002, p. 5)

Much of the latest brain research seeks to answer questions such as "How does the brain learn?" and "How do we remember?" The answers to these questions provide insights into learning, and therefore, teaching. This chapter explores the neurophysiology involved in learning, memory, and making connections.

It's All About Connections

Learning is about making connections. Brain-based research demonstrates that in order for teachers to have the fullest impact on their students, they must connect with students on two separate but overlapping levels: academic (content at grade level) and emotional (effective interpersonal interactions). In both cases, these connections have a neurological foundation that involves making new neural connections, strengthening existing neural connections, and creating neural networks, sometimes referred to as neural superhighways.

In the classroom, teachers make both academic and emotional connections with students. Academic learning is most likely the area you are most familiar with. For example, first-grade teachers expect to see entering students' reading and writing levels vary, ranging from below the first-grade level to the second-grade level, or above. The challenge is to put each child into the appropriate reading group, and then allow her to switch up or down as her learning occurs. These types of teaching decisions are familiar to us all.

The emotional, or interpersonal, level constitutes a relatively new level of focus in the classroom. Brain-based learning research clearly shows us the importance of making continual emotional connections with our students (Hardiman, 2003). In order for students to be able to learn new academic content, their "emotional brain" must tell them that it is both safe and important to learn the material (Hardiman, 2003). Chapter Eight discusses the role of emotion in greater depth, demonstrating that our emotions are intimately involved with learning and memory.

The remainder of this chapter is devoted to the examination of the neurophysiological components of learning.

Basic Brain Neurology

Some interesting brain facts: Our brain is a three-pound organ, give or take. If you put your two fists together, side-by-side, that is the approximate size of the brain. The brain's texture is that of a large, ripe avocado. It uses 20 percent of our body's energy, yet it makes up only 2 percent of our body's weight. Our brains are the home of our thoughts and our emotions. See Figure 2.1 for an illustration of the brain.

Since 1990, how the brain learns has been the focus of thousands of studies, articles, and books. The brain is truly the next scientific frontier, and there are vast areas inside our brain to explore.

Figure 2.1 The Brain

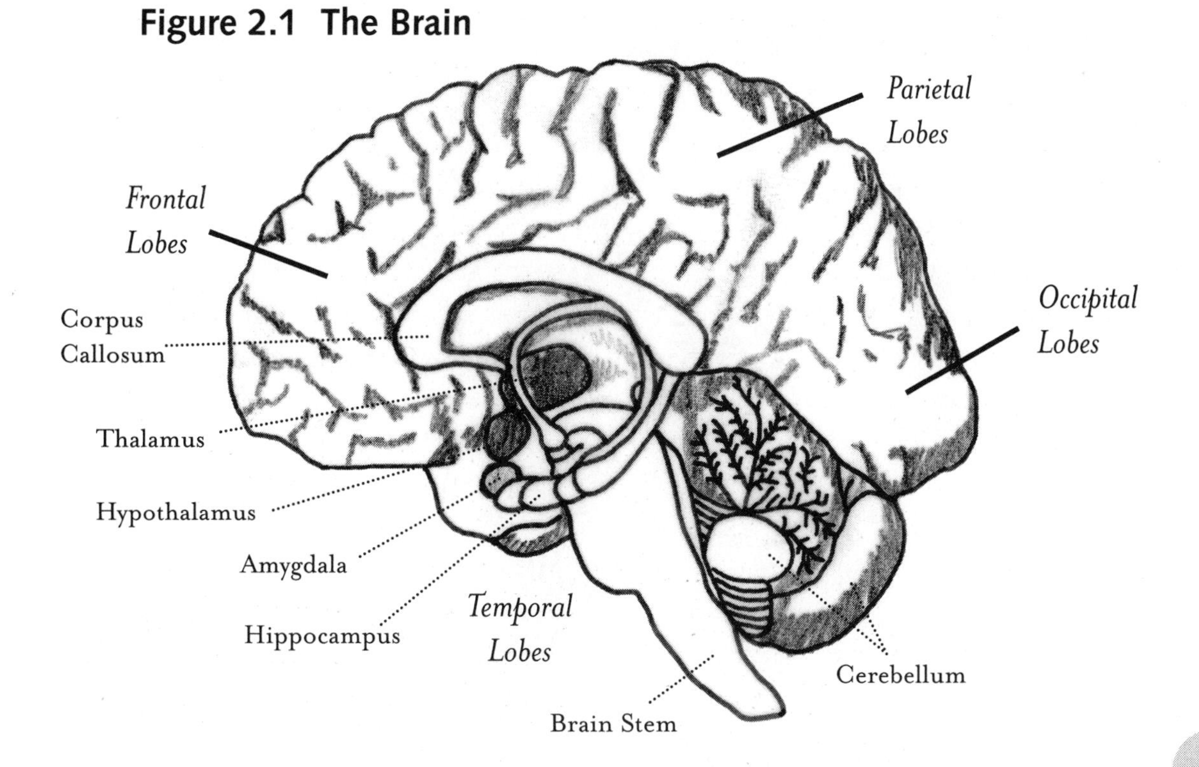

In *The Emotional Brain* (1996), neurologist Joseph LeDoux discusses how the human brain is the "product of evolutionary tinkering, where lots of little changes over extremely long periods of time have accumulated" (p. 104). At this very moment, our brain is in the process of evolving. LeDoux speculates that as the human brain continues to evolve, it is likely that human beings will strike a balance between our emotional centers and cognitive centers with a more "harmonious integration of reason and passion" (p. 303).

Brain-based educator Eric Jensen (1996) notes, "Our brain is prewired to learn what we need to learn to survive" (p. 6). Jensen believes that ensuring our survival is the most important function of the brain. It appears that our brain is designed to survive, and to adapt to whatever environment it is in, whether it is the rain forest, the tundra, or a modern American city.

The Triune Brain Theory

In 1969 Paul MacLean proposed an evolutionary theory of brain development called the Triune Brain Theory. This theory suggests that the human brain is actually composed of three brains that appeared at different stages in our evolution: the reptilian brain, which includes the brain stem and cerebellum, is the oldest; the limbic system, or the old mammalian brain, came next; and the neocortex, or the neomammalian brain, emerged most

Figure 2.2 Triune Brain Model

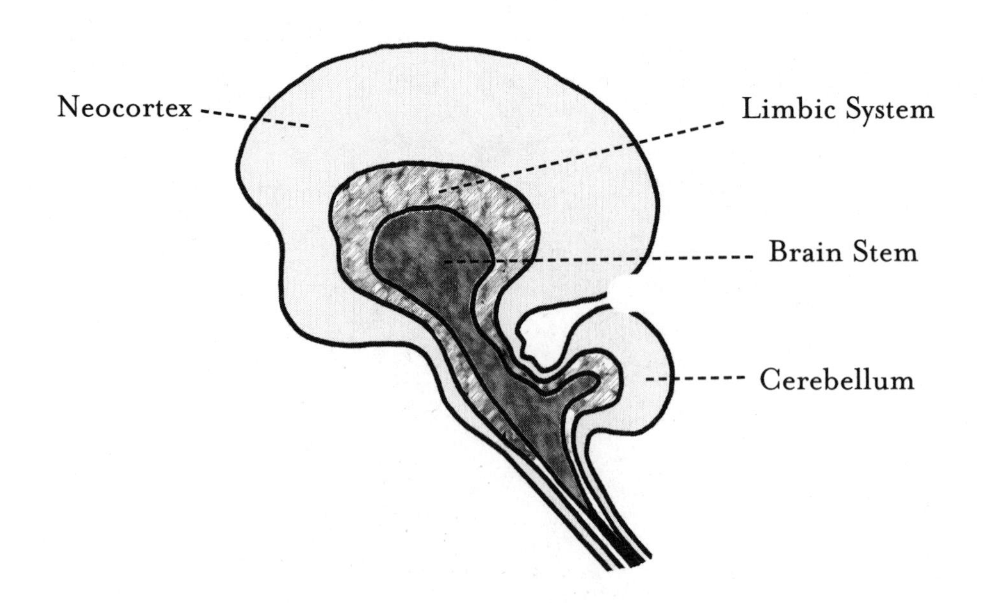

recently. (See Figure 2.2.) Each of these areas is separate, but they do not function independently.

According to MacLean's theory, the cerebellum and brain stem (see Figure 2.3) developed about 500 million years ago. Since it resembles the brain of reptiles and other early species, it is referred to as the reptilian brain. The reptilian brain is responsible for body functions needed for survival, such as heart rate and breathing. This ancient brain also determines our level of alertness; it warns us of important incoming information, such as a child riding a bicycle on our side of the road.

The limbic system (see Figures 2.4 and 2.5) was the second part of our brain to develop, about 250 million years ago. Since it corresponds to the brain of most mammals, it is often referred to as the mammalian brain. The key components of the limbic system are the amygdala, hippocampus, thalamus, and hypothalamus. This section of our brain is known primarily as the seat of our emotions. The limbic system is also responsible for regulating our appetite, sexual urges, sleeping, hormones, and our immune system. Our emotional brain will be discussed in depth in Chapter Eight.

Our neocortex, which is the outer part of the cerebrum (and which makes up about 85 percent of the human brain), was the last part of the brain to develop, about 200 million years ago. Reptiles do not have a neocortex and other mammals have only a small one. Our highly developed neocortex is the part of the brain that makes us human. It allows us to understand time—a sense of the past, present, and future. It allows us to reflect, to plan, and to make goals.

These three parts of our brain are distinct, but they interact and interconnect. The neocortex integrates information from the limbic system and the brain stem to plan, make decisions, and help us move.

Figure 2.3 The Brain Stem

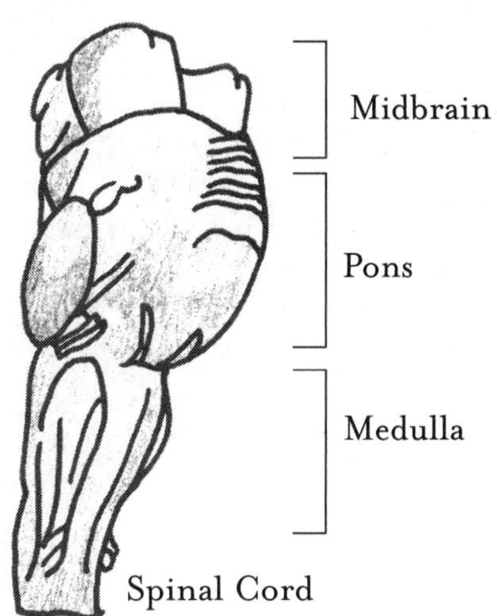

Figure 2.4 The Limbic System

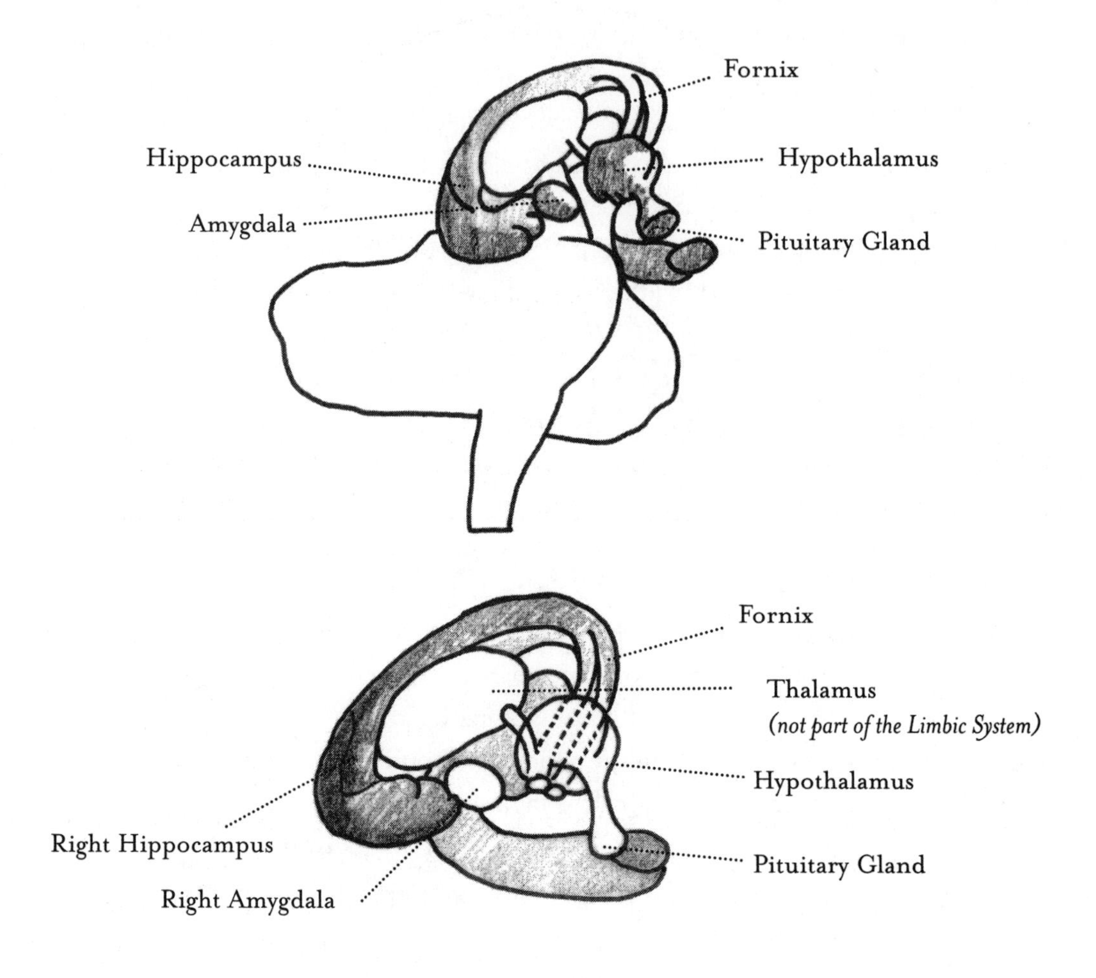

Figure 2.5 The Limbic System and Its Position in the Brain

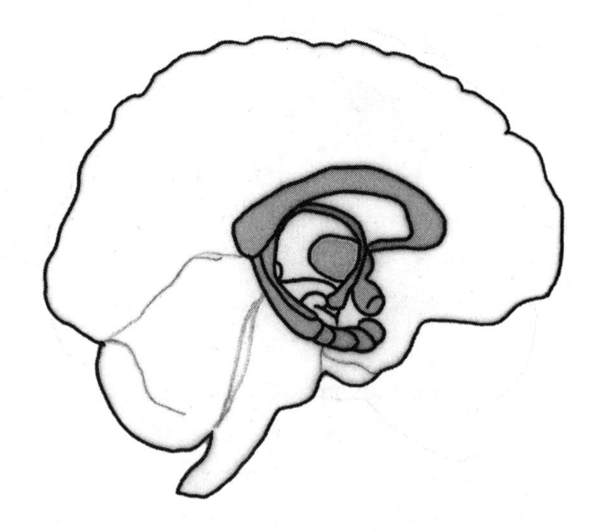

Figure 2.6 The Lobes of the Neocortex

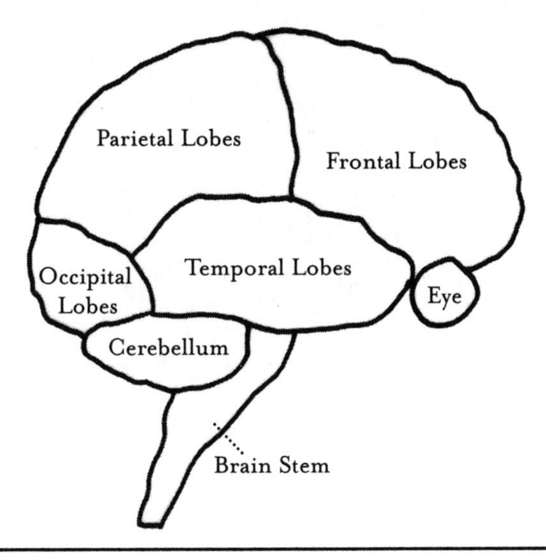

The Four Brain Lobes

The cerebrum (neocortex) is divided into two hemispheres, the left and right. These hemispheres are connected by a band of nerve cell fibers called the corpus callosum. The left and right hemispheres will be described in depth in Chapter Four. Both our left and right hemispheres house four highly developed areas called brain lobes (see Figure 2.6).

The frontal lobes make up the biggest section of the neocortex. From an evolutionary point of view, they were the last area of our brain to develop. The frontal lobes deal with planning for the future, decision-making, and problem-solving. They are located at the front of the brain, in our forehead area.

The temporal lobes have several functions. They deal with language reception, auditory processing, language comprehension, and speaking. The temporal lobes are located just above each ear.

Our occipital lobes are devoted to vision: how we see and process letters, shapes, and faces. They are sometimes referred to as our visual cortex. The occipital lobes are located at the back of the brain.

The left and right parietal lobes represent our body in the brain. They receive the incoming sensory information, and allow us to judge things like weight, shape, and texture. The parietal lobes are located at the top of our brain.

As the research makes clear, different areas of the brain are directly responsible for certain activities and behaviors. One result of this fact is that the brains of especially gifted people look different from the brains of others. People who are particularly good at a certain activity are highly developed in the related lobe. For example, a gifted writer or speaker may have an unusually well-developed left temporal lobe. A gifted artist is likely to have a well-developed right occipital lobe. Albert Einstein had well-developed parietal and frontal lobes. An autopsy of Einstein's brain showed that its total size and weight did not differ from brains of typical people. The difference was found in his parietal lobes, which were significantly larger than those of average people. The parietal lobes are the seat of mathematical and visual reasoning, two of the key elements in Einstein's type of thinking. When we say that an area of the brain is highly developed, we mean that within that lobe there are an unusually high number of neural connections among its cells. Neurologists who examined Einstein's brain found that his parietal lobes were about 15 percent wider than normal and unusually bulky, allowing for more neural interconnections among its cells. His large frontal lobes indicate that this area was used frequently to plan and problem solve.

The good news is that we can develop the different lobes in our brain. We can change our own brain and we can change our students' brains. For example, if we want to enhance our occipital lobes, we can take a pottery class. When we learn how to shape a vase with our hands, we increase the neural connections in our occipital lobes. If we want to enhance the occipital lobes of our students, we can add hands-on activities to our lectures. In other words, our brains undergo changes that are consistent with our skill level and experience.

Brain Cells

The brain is made up of two different types of cells: glial cells and neurons. The glial cells nurture the neurons, allowing them to work to their full potential. Glial cells are involved in the transportation of nutrients and help to regulate our immune system.

Neurologists and educators are most interested in the type of brain cells called neurons, or nerve cells. These are responsible for our learning. Neurons are able to receive, coordinate, analyze, and transmit information.

Neurons are sometimes referred to as the brain's computer chips. The power of a brain increases with the number of cells that it has in it. For example, a fruit fly has 100,000 brain cells, a mouse has 5 million, and a monkey has 10 billion. Humans, on the other hand, have 100 billion neurons. The numerous neurons in the human brain allow us to get out of the present moment in time; we are able to remember our past experiences and plan for the future.

What Are Neurons Made of and How Do They Work?

A neuron is a special type of cell that has three basic parts: dendrites, the cell body, and an axon (see Figure 2.7). A neuron can have many dendrites, but only one cell body and (usually) only one axon. A helpful analogy is to compare the nerve cell to a tree. The dendrites are the tree branches, the cell body is the top of the trunk where the branches begin to spread out, and the axon is the trunk of the tree. The trunk has a few roots in the ground called synaptic knobs or *telodendria*. These knobs do the actual message-sending.

Electrochemical information is passed between nerve cells in the form of substances called neurotransmitters. The nerve cells receive the information via the branchlike dendrites. These dendrites pass the information along to the cell body. Just as with the branches on a tree, dendrites (which is Greek for *trees*) have the capability to grow more appendages. The number of messages coming from the dendrites into the cell body helps to determine whether or not the cell will transmit messages to the axon, which is known as "firing."

Figure 2.7 Neuron

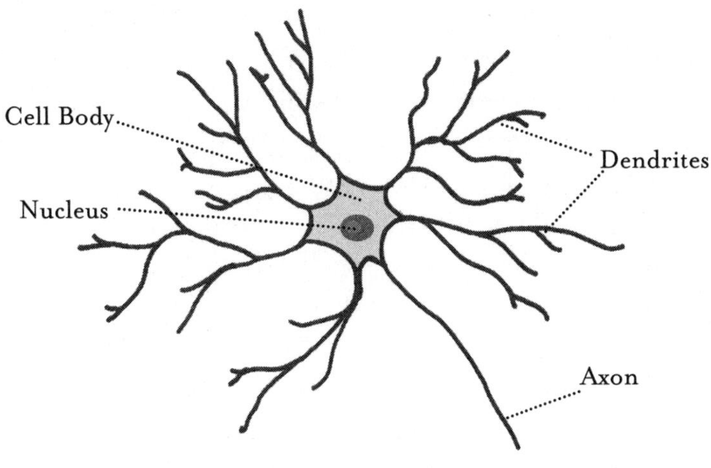

Figure 2.8 Communication Between Neurons

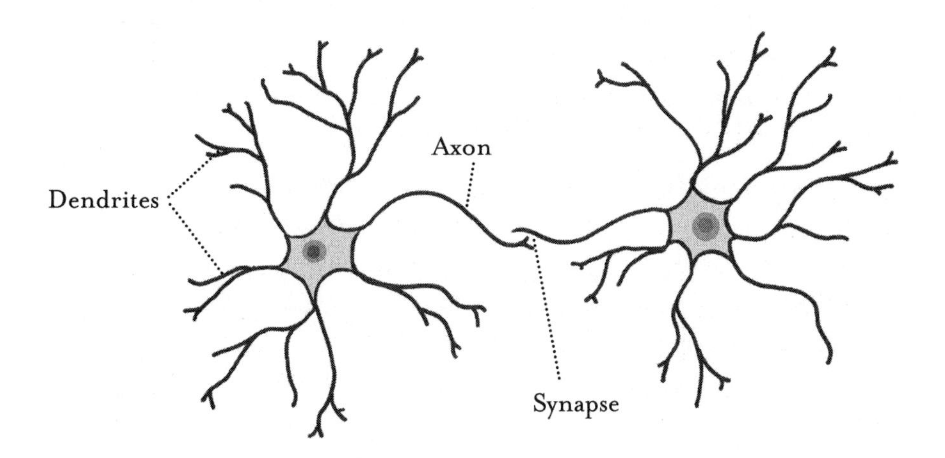

If the message does "fire," it moves from the cell body down the axon. It is important to note that in the case of neurons, communication is a one-way street. Axons speak only to dendrites, not to other axons. The most important function of an axon is to transport chemical substances and electrical information to other nerve cells.

There is, however, a very small space between nerve cells called a synapse. In order for nerve cells to pass along information, the electrical message must "swim" across this space, from the sending axon of the first neuron to the receiving dendrite of the next. These electrochemical processes take place at lightning speed. (See Figure 2.8.)

How Do We Learn?

Learning involves groups of neurons, or neural networks. One neuron is able to forge connections with up to 10 thousand other neurons. Our brains are capable of making approximately one million billion neural connections, and messages can travel along these passageways at speeds of up to 250 miles per hour (Jensen, 2000; Hardiman, 2003)! But how do we create new neural passageways in the brain?

When we first learn something new, it is slow going, similar to cutting a path for the first time in a large, dense forest. As we travel over the path time and time again, the same neurons are activated over and over. Essentially, we go from cutting the initial path through the forest to driving on a neural superhighway.

For example, consider the process of learning the alphabet. In preschool, students have to "cut down" a separate path for each letter. At first, it takes them a while to remember or recognize each letter. Usually, by the end of kindergarten, with a lot of practice, letter recognition comes easily, like speeding on a superhighway. In other words, the more we practice a skill, the stronger it gets; likewise, the more we use specific neural passageways, the stronger and more efficient they become. This is why educators strive for students to achieve automatic responses for letter recognition, letter sounds, and blends.

Learning Changes the Brain via Plasticity and Pruning

Our brains have a quality called "neural plasticity," which is the ability to learn and adapt (or relearn). Richard Restak (2001) notes that "plasticity is one of the fundamental principles of brain operation" (p. 38). For example, people can learn to live in different types of homes—wood houses, tents, or igloos. We can adapt to living in a cold climate in New England or a hot climate in Florida.

Neural plasticity is built into the human brain, giving it a remarkable capacity to reorganize itself, to make brain wiring more efficient, and to find compensatory neural pathways if there is a brain injury of some kind (Hardiman, 2003).

During the first two years of life, the brain makes neural connections at a very fast rate. The brain is connecting the infant to his body, making connections for sight, sound, touch, and movement. In addition, the brain is helping the baby make emotional connections with his primary caretakers.

At birth, a baby's brain has approximately 100 billion neurons. Not all of them are used during the baby's lifetime. In fact, "if neurons are not used at appropriate times during brain development, their ability to make connections dies" (Springer and Deutsch, 1998, p. 10). The neurons that are not used are "pruned" or eliminated. Pruning also eliminates redundant pathways and neural connections. The pruning of synapses occurs in each area of the brain, but at different times in different parts of the brain. For example, pruning in the areas devoted to vision occurs around four months of age, which makes sense developmentally, because at four months, a baby is beginning to recognize concrete objects. Pruning in the areas dealing with language comprehension occurs around three years of age.

As we grow and learn, the cells in our brain and our nervous system connect in complex patterns of neural pathways. Researchers believe that it takes at least until the age of 20 to complete the wiring of the brain. After 20, we still continue to make more brain connections through the enriching of our dendrites. It was long believed that after birth, no new neurons appeared. Only recently, however, scientists discovered that at least one area of the brain, the hippocampus, can, in fact, grow new neurons (Restak, 2001). So our brain changes throughout our lifetime, and can be enriched, and can even create new neurons.

Designing Our Own Neural Passageways

As we age, the covering around our neural axons, called the myelin sheath, grows thicker; see Figure 2.9. This improves the transmission of neuro-electrical connections in the brain. Our dendrites grow new branches, resulting in more interconnections for a richer, deeper, more profound type of

Figure 2.9 The Neuron

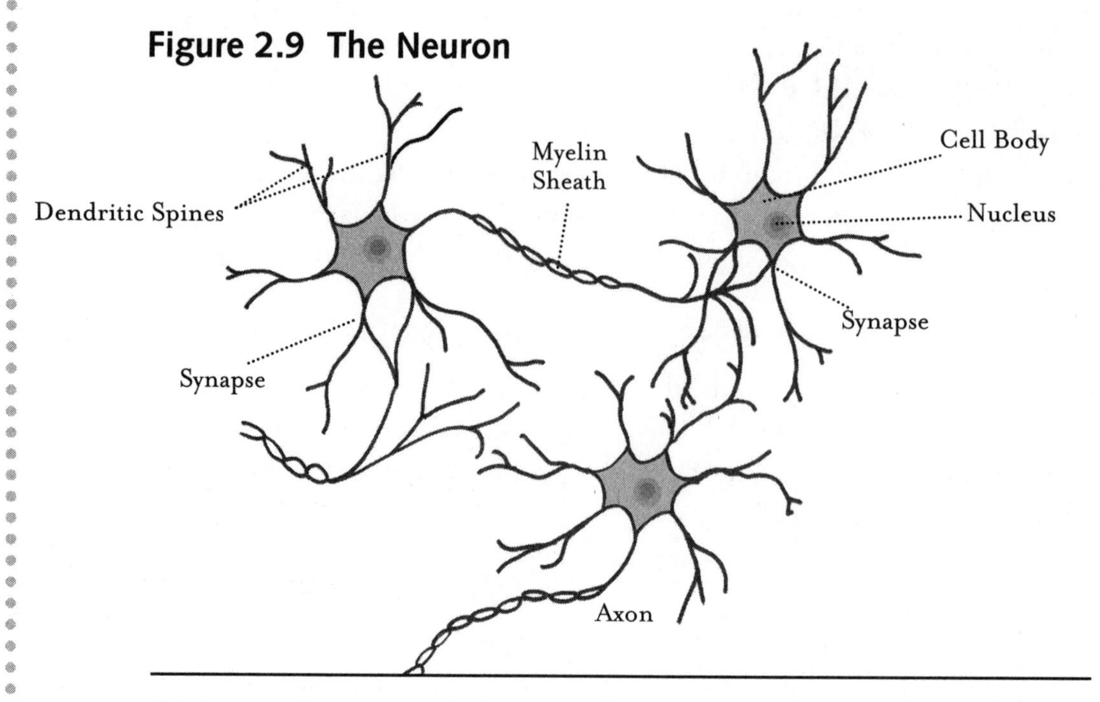

thinking. In fact, our frontal lobes are not fully developed until sometime in our early 20s, which helps explain why so many teenagers make misguided decisions. Around the age of 30, refinement of fine motor development in the hands and face occurs. This development can help musicians move their fingers more easily, and vocalists have more control over their vocal cords.

In a sense, as adults, we can virtually "design our own brain." We can choose what we read, what we study, our hobbies, and what graduate degree we want to pursue. With each new hobby, we, in essence, create new neural passageways. The more often the pathways are used, the stronger they become. Often our neural passageways intersect with one another, very much like a superhighway complete with bridges, overpasses, underpasses, rotaries, and the like. According to neurophysiologist Carla Hannaford (1995), we custom design our own nervous systems to meet the choices and challenges of our interests and livelihoods. In short, we are all in the process of becoming.

We now know that the brain is plastic and responsive. For teachers and learners, this is very good news. Now, let's turn to the ways in which the home and school environments affect the brain.

Chapter 3

Our Brain and Our Environment

"The bottom line is that experience changes the physiological structure and operation of our brains."

—Renate Caine and Geoffrey Caine (1994, p. 32)

Our experiences in life play a major role in shaping our brain. Both heredity and the environment affect the growth and the health of our brain. In Chapter Two, we discussed the neurological aspects (the inborn, hereditary side) of brain development. In this chapter we will examine how the environment is also a powerful force that serves to enrich, or damage, the brain.

Our day-to-day experiences change the physiological structure of our brain. An infant begins to experience life the moment she is born. Children who are picked up when they cry, fed when hungry, cuddled, and given hugs and warm blankets when they shiver learn that their basic needs will be met. When people experience pleasure, the limbic system conveys the message to the neocortex that the world is a safe and happy place. On the other hand, if our day-to-day experiences are full of rejection or neglect, the limbic system conveys the message to our neocortex that the world is frightening and unstable.

The good news is that parents and teachers can enhance the home and school environments to ensure optimal brain growth and development. We will begin this chapter with an examination of the key environmental factors found through brain research. This research presents some challenges for parents and teachers. Teachers are encouraged to create a safe and stimulating classroom environment. In so doing, we can help the brains of our students create new and enriched neural passageways. Abraham Maslow's theory of human motivation provides a foundation for our discussion.

Abraham Maslow's Hierarchy of Needs

Psychologist Abraham Maslow (1908–1970) is the founder of humanistic psychology. His work has had a profound impact on the psychology of motivation. At the core of his motivation theory is what he termed the "hierarchy of needs" (see Figure 3.1). According to this hierarchy, human beings are motivated to achieve physiological needs before being able to focus on emotional or spiritual needs. Maslow's hierarchy of needs provides a wonderful way to connect brain-based learning research to the needs of students in our classrooms.

Maslow believed that the lower-level needs of the hierarchy (physiological needs and safety) must be satisfied before higher-level needs (social, esteem, and self-actualization) can be pursued. The first four needs in Maslow's hierarchy are called "deficiency needs" because they result from what a person may lack. Once these needs are satisfied, the motivation for fulfilling them decreases. Maslow's three highest levels are called "growth needs" or "being needs," because they enhance our growth and development. The growth needs are never really satisfied or completed, because people seeking self-actualization activities find them intrinsically motivating and tend to continue them for the duration of their adult life. If events that satisfy our lower-level needs are disrupted, we can no longer focus on the higher levels. This applies to both children and adults.

You can see this clearly if you think about your own students. If a student comes to school without having her basic physiological needs met—if, for example, she's hungry or tired—she is certainly not able to concentrate on learning. Instead she will be inattentive, preoccupied with thoughts of food, or falling asleep.

As adults, we are less likely to be able to work as an effective team member when our spouse is out of work and we are worried about losing the house. In this case the majority of our energies must focus on basic concerns of such as selling our house, finding a smaller, less expensive place to live, seeing if we can remain in the same town, worrying about how to maintain our children's friends and activities.

Applying Maslow's Hierarchy in the Schools

We can apply Maslow's theory to our schools and to our individual classrooms. We know that the events in our students' lives directly influence their ability to learn. Many of these events, of course, are far outside our control. But when it comes to the classroom environment, we can have an

Figure 3.1 Maslow's Hierarchy of Needs

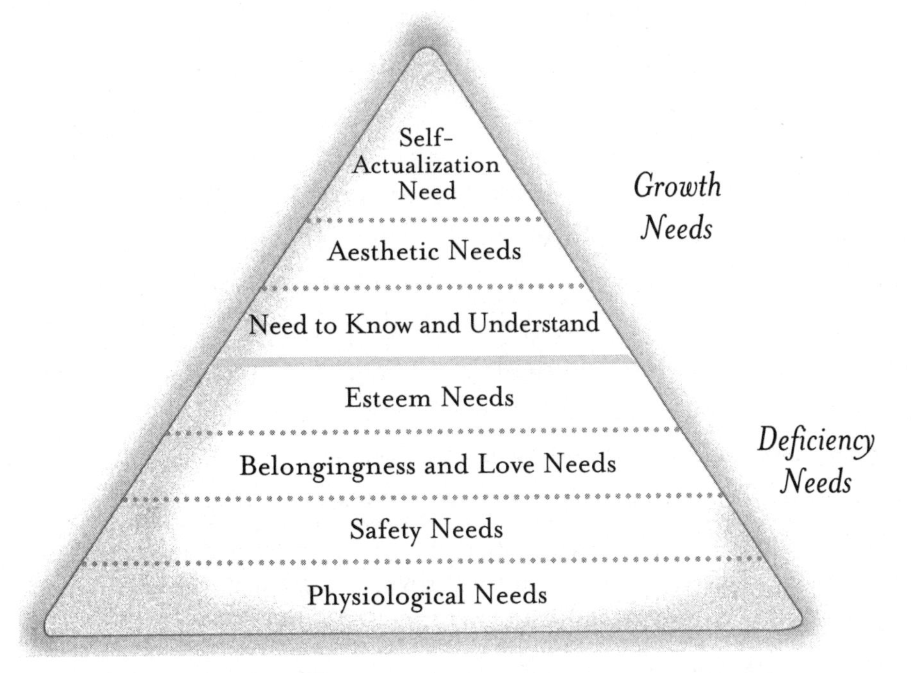

adapted from "A Theory of Human Motivation," Motivation and Personality (2nd ed.), *by A. Maslow, 1970, New York: Harper & Row, Publishers, Inc.*

impact. In Table 3.1, I've outlined each of Maslow's needs and suggested actions teachers and schools can take to help ensure those needs are met.

Maslow's hierarchy connects with current brain research in the following three ways. First, as Joseph LeDoux, a neurologist at New York University, has found, the human brain contains many neural passageways that run between our limbic brain and our neocortex. This finding is consistent with inclusion of both the emotions and the intellect inside Maslow's pyramid.

Second, neural information comes to our limbic system before it comes to our neocortex (LeDoux, 1996). This observation seems to mirror Maslow's idea that emotional needs must be addressed before cognitive needs (the need to know and the need to understand). It is noteworthy that esteem needs are placed before the cognitive needs in Maslow's hierarchy. This seems to suggest that it is our emotions that decide whether or not it is safe to pay attention and learn in school. In short, students' emotional and safety needs must be met before they can focus on their cognitive needs. It is clear that teachers need to address the emotional concerns of their students along with teaching the academic content.

Third, we see that once basic physical and cognitive needs are met, people move on to aesthetic appreciation and strive for self-actualization. As teachers, we should not neglect these needs but should offer challenging and stimulating work that addresses them, as Howard Gardner and Daniel Goleman have advocated.

Table 3.1 Correlations Between Maslow's Hierarchy of Needs and School Actions

Maslow's Hierarchy of Needs	Action
1. Physiological Needs	Provide free breakfast and lunch for those in need; give water breaks, give rest breaks for reflection.
2. Safety Needs	Provide a safe school environment, freedom from threat and/or harm; work with the bus drivers on safety issues.
3. Belongingness and Love Needs	Create feelings of belonging and community in school and classroom environments.
4. Esteem Needs	Recognize student goals and accomplishments, put projects on the walls and ceilings.
5. Need to Know and Understand	Assign some class work and homework in students' areas of strength; make assignments relevant to students' existing prior knowledge.
6. Aesthetic Needs	Provide challenging work that utilizes student creativity.
7. Self-Actualization Need	Provide challenging assignments that enable both innovation and self-reflection.

Environmental Factors That Enhance Brain Growth in Children and Adults

The home environment has a powerful influence on brain development in both animals and human beings. In 1988, neuroscientist Marian Diamond conducted a groundbreaking experiment with young rats. Some were raised in enriched environments where they had mazes to play in, toys, and a social environment (rat families and peers). Other rats were raised in impoverished environments in isolation from other rats, with no toys to stimulate their brains. The rats that were raised in the enriched environments developed fuller, richer dendrites in their cerebral cortex. Diamond found that after just one week, the cortexes of the rats in the enriched environment were 7 to 11 percent larger than the cortexes of the rats in the impoverished environment. Within two weeks, rats in the enriched environments developed 16 percent more extensive dendritic growth in the cerebral cortex, specifically in the frontal cortex and the visual-spatial areas of the brain.

In *Magic Trees of the Mind* (1998), Diamond discusses the ramifications for humans growing up in enriched versus impoverished environments.

Diamond reports that appropriate and varied environmental stimulation enables the human brain to make new dendritic connections, create new neural passageways, and/or strengthen existing ones.

Education consultants Renate and Geoffrey Caine (1994) write that we now know that "the physical structure of the brain changes as the result of experience" (p. 30). Children from enriched environments will come to school with more highly developed brains. The Caines describe enrichment as "a safe, consistent environment that provides opportunities for a variety of rich, emotional, social, and cognitive interactions" (p. 33). They suggest that "experiences actually shape our brains and, therefore, shape future learning. Thus, we use the brain better when we enrich our experiences so that our brains can extract new and more complex ways of communication and interacting with the world" (p. 39). Ronald Kotulak (1997) discusses the implications of the environment on our brain. He describes a longitudinal study conducted by Craig and Sharon Ramey that demonstrates that an enriched environment will enhance brain development in children. The Rameys used two groups of young children from an inner city. One group received an enriched environment that consisted of many learning experiences, good nutrition, children to play with, and toys; the other group used as a control group, remained at home and did not participate in an enriched environment. The Rameys tested the IQs of children in both groups after three years and found that the IQs of the children in the enriched group were 20 points higher than the IQs of the children in the control group. Kotulak writes that these findings should have a "revolutionary impact on early child-rearing practices and education, and provide further support for such intervention programs such as Head Start" (p. 52).

The following tables provide a partial summary of the environmental factors that can affect learning. Table 3.2 pertains to factors in the home environment; Table 3.3 refers to factors in the school environment that affect learning. Interestingly, all of these factors are within our ability to control, change, maintain, or enhance. Some of the most exciting implications of brain-based learning research are the opportunities the teacher has to create a brain-based learning environment in the classroom.

Each of the factors listed in Table 3.2 are worthy of consideration and exploration. The names of the researchers interested in each area are provided for those who wish to read further. Articles and books written by these researchers are listed in the bibliography.

In this chapter, I will discuss only two of these environmental factors: stress and prosody (our tone of voice). The need for classroom reflection is discussed in Chapter Seven.

Table 3.2 Brain-Based Environmental Factors

Environmental Factor	Reasons and Descriptions	Further Reading
1. A Loving Home Environment	Children who feel safe and are respected will be more willing to trust their own inclinations. When parents take time to listen to and play with their children, the children's limbic brain tells them that it is okay to try new activities.	William Pollack
2. An Enriched Home Environment	Offering a variety of activities to children will stimulate different areas of the brain (e.g., opportunities to play with other children; books, blocks, and puzzles in the home; opportunities to participate in sports and/or music activities; scouting groups; bike rides and family outings; art projects such as working with clay, crayons, paint, etc.)	Marilyn Diamond, Eric Jensen, Howard Gardner
3. A Daily Multivitamin for Children and Adolescents	Most people do not to obtain the necessary vitamins and minerals needed by the brain through food intake. Memory and attention are enhanced by vitamins.	Eric Jensen, Mary Anne Burkman and Katharina Streng
4. Balanced Diet and Nutrition	Proper nutrition is most easily obtained through three meals a day. Breakfast is especially important. Many children skip breakfast and do not get enough lean protein. Healthy snacks are also good for the brain.	Eric Jensen
5. Daily Exercise	Exercise has been found to "stimulate the growth of developing brains and prevent the deterioration of older brains." Exercise includes all activities including group sports, bike riding, roller blading, tennis, karate, skateboarding, walking, dancing, gymnastics, etc.	Carla Hannaford
6. Limited Television Viewing	New studies show a correlation between the amount of television watched per day and attention deficit disorder. Children who watch more television are more likely to be diagnosed with ADD.	Carla Hannaford

Table 3.3 Brain-Based School Environmental Factors

Environmental Factor	Reasons and Descriptions	Further Reading
1. Safe Classroom Environment	Before our students' neocortex will take in and learn new information, their limbic system must tell the neocortex that it is "safe" to learn. Students will feel that it is safe to learn when teachers enforce rules that all students are to be respected at all times regardless of multicultural differences or learning differences.	Diane Connell and Betsy Gunzelmann, William Pollack
2. Stimulating/ Challenging Classroom Environment	Changing the classroom environment during the day (e.g., whole group, small group, one-on-one) will enable different parts of the brain to be stimulated.	Eric Jensen, Diane Connell, Carla Hannaford
3. Varied Teaching Methods	Presenting material using different types of learning styles during the day (using as many multiple intelligences as possible in a lesson; varying left-brain versus right-brain approaches; using visual, auditory, and kinesthetic activities) will enable different parts of the brain to be stimulated and new neural connections to be formed.	Eric Jensen, Howard Gardner, Diane Connell and Betsy Gunzelmann, Carla Hannaford
4. Teacher's Tone of Voice (Prosody)	Our students hear and process both our spoken and our unspoken messages. Expressing genuine encouragement, and showing our excitement when we teach new (and old) material works wonders on our students' limbic system. Their limbic system informs the neocortex that it is "time to learn!"	James Zull
5. Teacher's Hand, Facial, and Other Gestures	Approximately 65 percent of communication is nonverbal. Our students' limbic system interprets our messages in order to determine if it is safe to learn; and, if the information is relevant for them to learn.	Sue Thompson, James Zull
6. Encouraging Students to Drink Water	Human brains need three to five glasses daily of water to function optimally. Our bodies attempt to maintain a balance between salt intake and water. Drinks containing caffeine (coffee, tea, soda), salt, and sugar (fruit juices, soda) tend to cause dehydration, which depletes the water supply in our body and brain. Dehydration can cause headaches and decrease our learning potential. The brain needs a constant water supply to produce protective cerebrospinal fluid.	Eric Jensen, Carla Hannaford

Table 3.3 Brain-Based School Environmental Factors *continued*

7. Providing Movement Throughout the Day	Exercise increases the supply of blood and oxygen to the brain.	Carla Hannaford
8. Nonfluorescent Lighting	Fluorescent lights have a "hum" that can raise the cortisol levels in the blood. Cortisol is the hormone that is released when we are stressed.	Wayne London, Eric Jensen
9. Reduced Stress	Constant stress negatively affects the brains of our students. (See discussion below.)	James Zull, Daniel Goleman
10. Time for Reflection Throughout the Day	Reflection time is needed to give our brain time to search for, and develop, stronger neural connections.	James Zull

A Closer Look at Prosody

James Zull (2002) refers to prosody as "the other side of language," meaning the "emotional side" of language. Neurologically speaking, we process language using both cognitive and emotional neural passageways. In essence, the cognitive aspects of the words we hear or read are processed in our left hemisphere in the left temporal lobe. Our right hemisphere processes the emotional aspects of the contents of the words in the right temporal lobe. The right hemisphere processes the tone, the rhythm, the pitch, and the inflection of the words. These aspects of language are called prosody, and they are significant for understanding the meaning of the words. The functions of our left and right hemispheres will be described in depth, in the next chapter.

For years, I have been thinking about the effect tone of voice has on others. I have a friend of 30 years, Mary Raddock, who lives four hours from me. Our most frequent means of communication is the telephone. Over the years, I have noted that she consistently manages to sound positive and enthusiastic in these phone conversations. These qualities are part of her personality, but how is this zeal conveyed through her voice via the telephone. What brain dynamics are taking place?

When Mary is talking with me, I hear the cadence in her voice. The communication that comes to my emotional limbic brain is "Mary's messages are dependable, exciting and stimulating"—it is good and safe to listen to her. The messages that the limbic brain sends to my neocortex are "Listen. Think. Interact."

On the other hand, there is a man I know whose tone is often angry and impatient. When he is speaking with me in this tone, I tend to take a step back emotionally. What is happening neurophysiologically? When I am around this particular man, my emotional limbic system is telling me "It's not safe; protect yourself." My limbic system takes some of the blood and oxygen out of my neocortex to "protect me," and to get me ready for a possible fight-or-flight situation. In this semisurvival mode, I am more tuned into his tone than to his words. I often leave these interactions feeling bad and not cognitively sure of what was said.

Teachers can use prosody to convey feelings such as excitement about content, as well as feelings of acceptance regarding students' questions and responses. Zull (2002) writes, "I suspect that a great deal of the art of changing the brain has to do with the effective use of prosody. Teachers who convey deeper meaning by their powers of expression, both semantic and prosodic, have a better chance to reach their students" (p.172). When I teach, I consciously use my voice to convey the excitement I feel when I am talking about topics. Some say that teaching requires a bit of acting. We may have to project if we want our students to know that it is truly important to learn what we are teaching them. Chances are, when we convey enthusiasm about our topic, students will feel this enthusiasm, and get excited as well. I suggest that we use the power of prosody in our classrooms.

The Classroom Implications of Stress

If for some reason, we come across to our students as angry, impatient, or uncaring, their brains will do the same thing my brain does when I speak with the man mentioned above: namely, shift into a fight-or-flight stance. When stressed, students cannot learn the academic content being offered because their limbic system is pulling the blood and oxygen away from their neocortex. When stressed, our heart rate increases, and our adrenal gland secretes the stress hormone cortisol into the blood.

Goleman (1998) notes, "Cortisol steals energy resources from the working memory. . . . When cortisol levels are high, people make more errors, are more distracted, and can't remember as well. Irrelevant thoughts intrude, and processing information becomes more difficult" (p. 76). Zull (2002) explains, "High cortisol levels in the bloodstream can damage cells in the hippocampus and even kill them. Extreme stress can permanently damage our memory centers; this effect has been implicated in cases of extreme depression and in post traumatic stress disorder" (p. 83).

It is clear that if a student is stressed, he or she will not be able to learn efficiently, and perhaps not at all. Certainly a harsh tone of voice is only one small cause of stress in our students. Stress is also caused by many different unpleasant situations at home or at school or in the environment at large. Needless to say, as teachers, we want to strive to make our classrooms as stress-free as possible.

Creating a Safe Classroom

When the teacher is perceived as loving, happy, and enthusiastic, this emotional information also goes directly to the students' limbic brain. This time, though, the limbic brain says, "It is safe to relax, listen, and learn." When our students feel safe, information flows from the limbic system to the neocortex, and learning can take place. This, of course, is the atmosphere we need to actively strive for as much as possible.

Stress-Reducing Strategies

There are a number of easy stress-reducing strategies you can teach your students. Here are a few you might wish to try.

Yoga

Teachers who know yoga often use simple exercises in the classroom to help students alleviate stress either before a test or when they seem especially anxious. The basic idea is that if our students are feeling peaceful and relaxed, they will be able to put forth their best effort on the task ahead, whether it's a classroom test, a state exam, or acting in a school play. If you are not familiar with yoga yourself, you can visit one of several Web sites for more information. On www.yogakids.com, Darlene Paris has posted Teaching Yoga to Kids. She explains that yoga can be used in conjunction with reading, writing, storytelling, poetry, and music and is used to build self-confidence. On www.childrensyoga.com/sharing.htm, there are links called "teacher sharing" and "teacher training." On the "teacher sharing" link, Elaina Sharp, an occupational therapist, writes that yoga has provided children with "important tools to use to decrease anxiety, increase self-awareness, and learn to self calm."

Breathing Exercises

Breathing or "centering" exercises are easy-to-do activities that quickly elicit states of relaxation and calm. The neurological explanation for why these exercises induce relaxation is that they increase the production of neurotransmitters and shift the brain to the lower alpha and theta brain wave frequencies. In addition, deep-breathing exercises provide extra oxygen to the blood and brain, causing the brain to release endorphins. Endorphins are naturally occurring chemicals in the body that lift mood, reenergize the body, and promote relaxation. Needless to say, these centering exercises are advantageous for teachers as well, both inside and outside of the classroom.

To perform a basic breathing exercise with your students, follow these instructions:

1. Have students sit comfortably with their eyes closed.
2. Encourage them to relax and to focus their attention on their breathing.
3. Ask them to breathe in through the nose, slowly expanding their abdomen as they do so.
4. Instruct them to exhale slowly through the mouth.

Once this breathing is mastered, you might encourage students to visualize a peaceful thought, or to create a picture in their mind of a beautiful place. This process can produce effective results in only two to three minutes.

Brain Gym

A growing number of K–12 teachers are using Brain Gym activities in their classroom. Brain Gym exercises utilize a combination of our mind and body. According to Carla Hannaford (1995), Brain Gym facilitates each step of the learning process and brings it to learning readiness. Hannaford explains that the Brain Gym exercises activate "full mind/body function through simple integrative movements, which focus on specific aspects of sensory activation and facilitate integration of function across the body midline" (p. 112).

One Brain Gym activity is called the Cross Crawl. To perform the Cross Crawl, stand in place and slowly touch the right elbow to the left knee, and then touch the left elbow to the right knee. The knees are picked up and put down in a type of slow march. This activity is done slowly, and like all Brain Gym activities, it is advisable to drink water before and after the exercise.

What does the Cross Crawl do to stimulate the brain? Hannaford explains that the Cross Crawl "is like consciously walking, which facilitates balanced nerve activation across the corpus callosum. When done on a regular basis, more nerve networks form and myelinate in the corpus callosum, thus making communication between the two hemispheres faster and more integrated for high-level reasoning" (p.119). In other words, this activity forces the body to cross its midline (middle), and in so doing, it activates full brain function via the corpus callosum to help neural material cross back and forth between the left and right hemispheres. (For more on brain hemispheres, see Chapter Four.) Doing the Cross Crawl slowly is important because the slowness "requires more fine motor involvement and balance, consciously activating the vestibular system and the frontal lobes" (Hannaford, 1995, p. 119). Fine motor involvement activates the vestibular system (in the inner ear) and the frontal lobes. To find out about other Brain Gym activities, you can read *Smart Moves—Why Learning Is Not All in Your Head* by Carla Hannaford, or go to the Brain Gym Web site at www.braingym.com.

Looking Ahead

In the following chapters, we'll explore the question "Who Am I?" and examine the implications for our teaching. I present different leading theories about the how the brain is organized and how we learn. Each of these theories provides a different lens through which to view yourself and your students; however, the theories complement each other and can be used together to create a full, well-rounded image of yourself and those you teach.

In Chapter Four you'll find out whether you and your students are left-, right-, or middle-brained. In Chapter Five, you and your students will determine your strong, moderate, and least-developed intelligences. Chapters Six and Seven should be considered in tandem: In Chapter Six we delve into the fascinating theory of information processing; Chapter Seven explores how these processes affect our learning styles. Then, in Chapter Eight, we'll consider emotional intelligence. You'll find exploratory questionnaires, as well as some ideas to create an emotional climate that's conducive to learning.

Chapter 4

Are You Left-, Right-, or Middle-Brained?

"Every brain simultaneously perceives and creates parts and wholes."

—Renate Caine, Geoffrey Caine, and Sam Crowell (1999, p. 127)

Sam, a fourth-grade student, starts to draw every time I teach a new concept or explain an assignment. Why isn't he listening to me?

Dorothy says that she feels ill every time I begin an art lesson. She asks to go see the nurse. Why doesn't she enjoy art as much as the other children do?

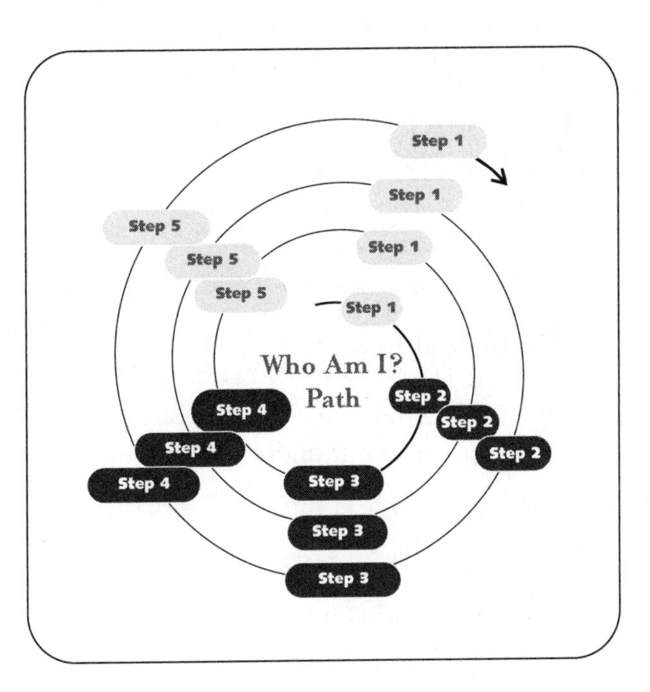

Interestingly, the answers to the questions posed by these scenarios lie in first knowing ourselves as teachers, understanding our teaching styles, and then striving to understand the learning styles of our students. One way to do this is to understand how our "neurological style" influences the way we teach.

We process sensory information using a left-, a right-, or a middle-brain preference.

The left-brain/right-brain theory provides one extremely interesting and useful way to know ourselves and our students. The left-brain/right-brain theory described by Sally Springer and Georg Deutsch (1998) in *Left Brain, Right Brain: Perspectives from Cognitive Neuroscience* constitutes the first stop on the "Who Am I?" path. Let's examine some of the theoretical underpinnings of this theory.

Left-, Right-, and Middle-Brain Theory and Research

The brain is divided into two halves, called hemispheres, both of which play a role in determining how we process information, and how we think, learn, and act; see Figure 4.1. Each hemisphere has a specific function and works in a distinct way. The left hemisphere processes information in a sequential, analytical manner; the right hemisphere processes information in a more holistic and intuitive manner. Following is a general description of the function of each hemisphere of the brain.

Left-brain functions:

- Constantly monitors our sequential, ongoing behavior
- Responsible for awareness of time, sequence, details, and order
- Responsible for auditory receptive and verbal expressive strengths
- Specializes in words, logic, analytical thinking, reading, and writing
- Responsible for boundaries and knowing right from wrong
- Knows and respects rules and deadlines

Right-brain functions:

- Alerts us to novelty; tells us when someone is lying or making a joke
- Specializes in understanding the whole picture
- Specializes in music, art, visual-spatial and/or visual-motor activities
- Helps us form mental images when we read and/or converse
- Responsible for intuitive and emotional responses
- Helps us to form and maintain relationships

In Chapter Two we discussed that neurons have an electrochemical basis. Several instruments have been designed that can record small changes in the brain's electrical activity or "brain waves." Brain waves can be recorded by a small metal disk attached to the scalp. The record is called an electroencephalogram (EEG). Other devices that are used to take images of the brain include the computerized tomography (CT scan), the positron-emission tomography (PET), the magnetic resonance imaging (MRI), and the functional MRI (fMRI) (Kolb and Whishaw, 2000). Neurologists have studied brain waves to aid in diagnosing epilepsy and brain damage, as well as for studying normal brain behavior, including sleep patterns and for monitoring depths of anesthesia.

Electroencephalograms (EEGs) have been used to record the electrical activity of the brain. Studies on infants just two hours old show that when babies hear words, parts of their left brain "light up"; when the same babies hear music, parts of their right brain "light up." These studies confirm that each of our brain hemispheres has a different information-processing style. In other words, our left and right hemispheres use completely different strategies when trying to solve a problem.

Springer and Deutsch (1998) explain that those who are left-brain dominant are guided by the analytical, time-oriented left hemisphere. The left hemisphere responds most strongly to auditory input; in other words, it tunes into words, voices, and verbal messages. Left-brain characteristics include an awareness of time, sequence, details, and order. It is a focus on the trees (the details), not the forest (the big picture). The left hemisphere prefers the rules of algebra to the spatial forms of geometry. Left-brain people tend to process information by paying attention to facts and words, as opposed to pictures or touch.

Figure 4.1 Hemispheres of the Brain

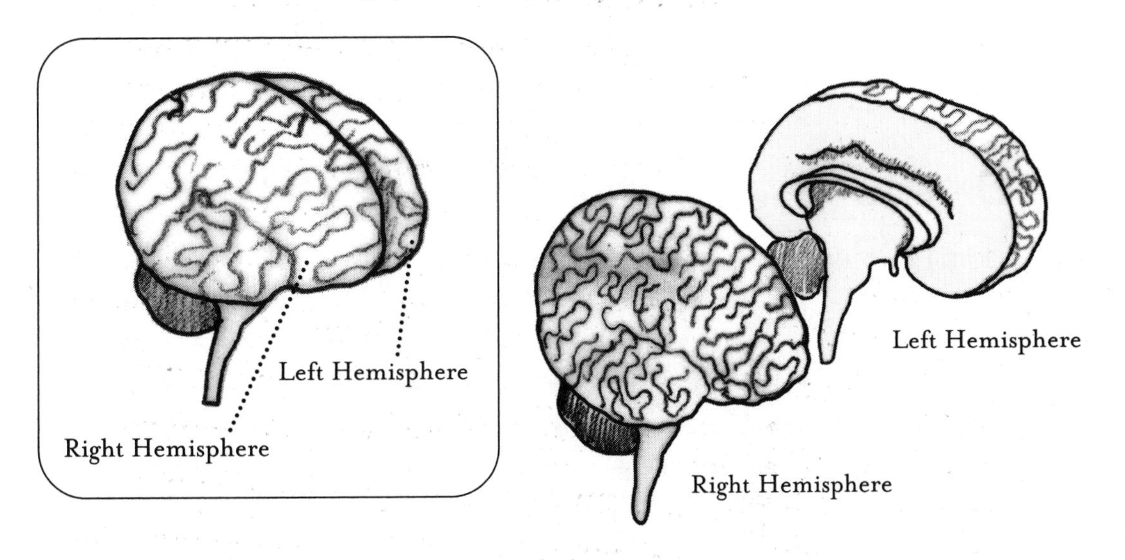

Our abilities to understand and speak language are organized in the left hemisphere. The left temporal lobe houses two areas devoted to understanding and expressing language: Wernicke's area and Broca's area. Wernicke's area specializes in receiving auditory information from the environment. Broca's area is the part of the brain that allows us to express ourselves verbally. Neurological damage to Broca's area results in aphasia, which is the inability to speak correctly in spite of intact vocal mechanisms.

In contrast, individuals with a right-brain dominance, process information primarily visually; they most easily learn by processing pictures or graphs (Semrud and Hynd, 1990). The right hemisphere makes intuitive leaps to quickly understand a sensation, and processes information without consideration of time.

Our right hemisphere alerts us to novelty by telling us when someone is lying or making a joke. Right-brain characteristics include spatial awareness and an ability to create with our hands; in fact, the right brain specializes in eye-hand or visual-motor activities. In the mind's eye we can visualize how a product should look when it is finished, and then follow through with our hands to create artwork, woodwork, sculptures, knitting, pottery and/or architectural blueprints. Visual-motor and visual-spatial strengths can result in an orientation toward sports, painting, and sculpture.

Right-brain, visual-spatial abilities also help us form mental images when we read, converse, and hear jokes. Geometry is easier than algebra for most right-brain people.

Whether you are left- or right-brain dominant, or middle-brained (which means neither hemisphere is dominant), you possess and use the functions from both hemispheres; however, we are all influenced by our neurological strengths. For example, when you solve a problem, do you tend to be more analytical or more intuitive? Do you like to reflect before you act, or are you more spontaneous? Your actions reflect your brain preferences, which in turn affect your teaching style.

Determining Your Left-/Right-/Middle-Brain Preference

Loren D. Crane of Western Michigan University devised the Alert Scale of Cognitive Style in 1989 to help people discover their left- and right-brain preferences. Take the Alert Scale on pages 43–44 to see what your brain preference is, then we'll discuss the implications for your teaching. Tally your results to learn whether you are a left-, right-, or middle-brain teacher.

Alert Scale of Cognitive Style

Choose the one sentence that is more true. Do not leave any blanks.

1. A. It's fun to take risks.
   B. I have fun without taking risks.

2. A. I look for new ways to do old jobs.
   B. When one way works well, I don't change it.

3. A. I begin many jobs that I never finish.
   B. I finish a job before starting a new one.

4. A. I'm not very imaginative in my work.
   B. I use my imagination in everything I do.

5. A. I can analyze what is going to happen next.
   B. I can sense what is going to happen next.

6. A. I try to find the one best way to solve a problem.
   B. I try to find different answers to problems.

7. A. My thinking is like pictures going through my head.
   B. My thinking is like words going through my head.

8. A. I agree with new ideas before other people do.
   B. I question new ideas more than other people do.

9. A. Other people don't understand how I organize things.
   B. Other people think I organize well.

10. A. I have good self-discipline.
    B. I usually act on my feelings.

11. A. I plan time for doing my work.
    B. I don't think about the time when I work.

Source: The Alert Scale of Cognitive Style *by Dr. Loren D. Crane, Western Michigan University, 1989. Reprinted with permission.*

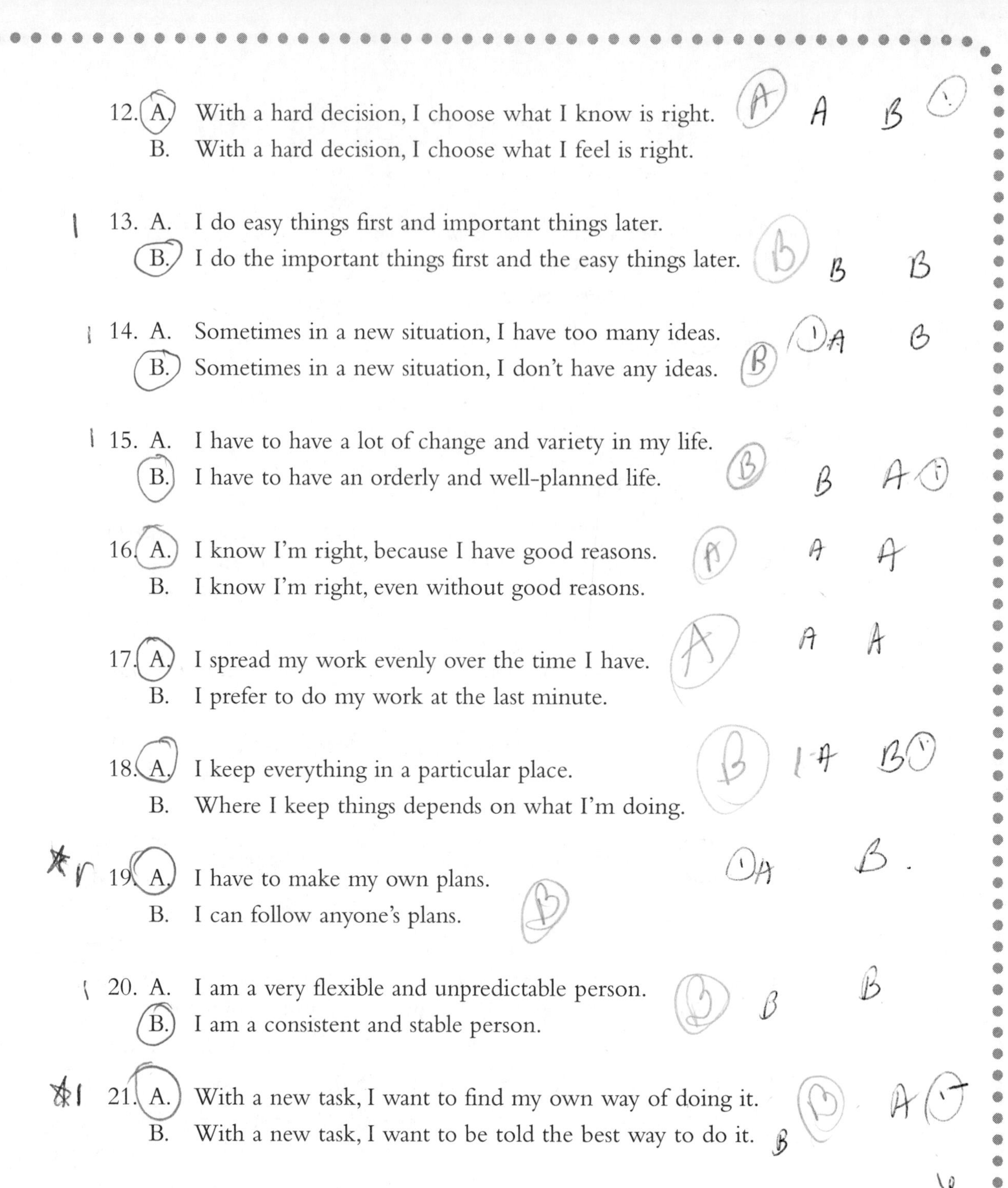

12. A. With a hard decision, I choose what I know is right.
    B. With a hard decision, I choose what I feel is right.

13. A. I do easy things first and important things later.
    B. I do the important things first and the easy things later.

14. A. Sometimes in a new situation, I have too many ideas.
    B. Sometimes in a new situation, I don't have any ideas.

15. A. I have to have a lot of change and variety in my life.
    B. I have to have an orderly and well-planned life.

16. A. I know I'm right, because I have good reasons.
    B. I know I'm right, even without good reasons.

17. A. I spread my work evenly over the time I have.
    B. I prefer to do my work at the last minute.

18. A. I keep everything in a particular place.
    B. Where I keep things depends on what I'm doing.

19. A. I have to make my own plans.
    B. I can follow anyone's plans.

20. A. I am a very flexible and unpredictable person.
    B. I am a consistent and stable person.

21. A. With a new task, I want to find my own way of doing it.
    B. With a new task, I want to be told the best way to do it.

Scoring

Give yourself one point for each time you answered "A" for questions: 1, 2, 3, 7, 8, 9, 13, 14, 15, 19, 20, 21
Give yourself one point for each time you answered "B" for questions: 4, 5, 6, 10, 11, 12, 16, 17, 18
Add all points

0–4 strong left brain	14–16 moderate right brain
5–8 moderate left brain	17–21 strong right brain
9–13 middle brain	

Source: The Alert Scale of Cognitive Style *by Dr. Loren D. Crane, Western Michigan University, 1989. Reprinted with permission.*

Understanding Your Results

Now that you've got your results, what does it mean? How can this understanding affect your teaching?

Left-Brain Dominant

If you are left-brain dominant, it is your left hemisphere that guides how you think, what you believe, and how you make decisions. Our left hemisphere is aware of time in the past, present, and future and uses this information to make decisions. It monitors our routine, ongoing behavior, and likes to process information in a sequential manner. It is our left brain that gets us out of bed in the morning, dressed, fed, out the door, and to school on time.

Left-brain teachers often know that they are left-brained once they hear the two hemispheres described. For example, school teachers with a left-brain dominance will say something similar to what Frank, a middle-school science teacher wrote: "I am certain that I am left brain because I like to lecture. I like doing the research to prepare my lectures, and I expect my students to listen quietly and take notes." Here's a comment from another left-brain teacher named Carla, a third-grade teacher: "I need to have order in my day. Each morning the daily schedule is on the board. In order to get all of my goals accomplished, I follow this schedule precisely, giving my students five-minute notices when we are about to change from arithmetic to spelling." It's true that left-brain teachers prefer to teach using structured lectures, and prefer giving assignments and activities such as research papers, debates, and book reports that are written as opposed to presented or drawn.

Psychologically, our left brain provides us with boundaries and a sense of knowing right from wrong. It is in charge of the "shoulds." I "should" hold my temper when Sam starts to draw; I "should" believe that Dorothy is getting sick when we have art. Our left hemisphere knows and respects rules and deadlines. Left-brain people tend to be annoyed when others are late. They tend to be reserved and have a tendency to speak after thinking. The left hemisphere gives us our sense of separateness and individuality.

Right-Brain Dominant

If you are right-brain dominant, it is your intuitive, emotional right hemisphere that guides the decisions you make throughout the day. The right brain specializes in processing a lot of information simultaneously by seeing the whole picture. Our right hemisphere sees the forest, not the trees. It tunes into feelings, music, art, and sports.

When they learn about the left-brain/right-brain distinctions, most right-brain teachers know they are right-brained both in their personal and professional lives. Caitlin, a third-grade teacher, writes, "Although I start each day with plans, I allow the students extra time to finish their projects whenever they need it. I think that as a society we rush too much, and I refuse to rush my students. I know I am right brain because time is not as important to me as perfecting the final product." Betsy, a right-brain middle-school geography teacher, describes the importance of hands-on projects. She writes, "I prefer not to lecture too much to the students; rather I enjoy thinking up projects for them to create. Students learn best when they can work together to make projects such as posters or maps. My room is full of materials that the students are encouraged to use on a daily basis. I am also a photographer, and I bring this skill into the classroom by encouraging my students to use photographs or pictures along with their written materials."

It is true that right-brain teachers tend to lecture less than their left-brain counterparts. I know when I enter the room of a right-brain teacher—it has colorful projects hanging from the ceiling and on the walls, wonderful bulletin boards, and an abundance of art materials. The day is dominated more by lively group projects and less by teacher presentations.

Psychologically, our right brain is intuitive and emotional. It allows us to get deeply involved in a project and causes us to lose track of time. It is accepting of differences, and can see both sides of a situation. Our right brain is in command of the "coulds." I "could" just let Sam draw while I lecture; I "could" work with Dorothy and the guidance counselor to help her deal with her fear of failing at art. Our right hemisphere helps us to form and maintain relationships; it provides a sense of "we." Right-brain people tend to be aware of and share their feelings more frequently than left-brain-dominant people.

Middle-Brained

While many people have a dominant left or right side of the brain, there are some who would be considered middle-brained. Those whose strengths are more or less equally distributed throughout both hemispheres fall into the middle-brain range (Crane, 1989). These people tend to be more flexible with how tasks are carried out than either the left- or the right-brain-dominant person. In a sense, middle-brain people are more balanced than either left- or right-brain people. They are able to see a problem and solve it from different perspectives. However, they can be indecisive because, neurologically, they can do most tasks through either a left- or a right-brain method (Connell, 2002).

Many middle-brain people feel that although they should be classified as middle-brained, they believe that they lean either toward the left or toward the right. For example, I have heard middle-brain teachers say something along the lines of what Sheri told me: "I can see that I am middle brain because I am a very good writer and very good at designing hands-on projects for the students, but I think I lean more toward the right because I am readily in touch with my feelings. . . . I feel more than I think." Others, like Roberta, lean to the left: "I do believe that I am truly middle brain. I like to be alone (left) and I like to be with people (right). I can organize big parties but I do it in a step-by-step manner. In a crisis, I will think my way through it . . . so I believe that in the final analysis, I am middle brain, but I tug to the left."

Middle-brain teachers tend to be the most flexible teachers. When I observe their classrooms, I see elements of both left- and right-brain processing.

Interpreting Your Results From a Teaching Perspective

You now know whether your preference tends to be left, right, or middle brain, but what does this mean for you as a teacher? First, for those of you who came out to be either strong to moderate left- or right-brain dominant, be assured that your other hemisphere is alive and well; however, the results do mean that, as a teacher, you tend to make decisions most often through your dominant hemisphere.

The Left-Brain Teacher

Teachers with left-brain strengths prefer to teach using lecture and discussion. To incorporate sequence, they put outlines on the chalkboard or the overhead, and adhere to prepared time schedules. They give problems to the students to solve independently. Teachers with left-brain preferences assign more research and more writing assignments than their right-brain peers. A reasonably quiet classroom with structure (desks lined up) is preferred. The classroom tends to be orderly with items in their places.

The Right-Brain Teacher

In contrast, teachers with right-brain strengths prefer to use hands-on activities as opposed to lecture. In concert with the right-brain tendency of seeing the whole picture, these teachers incorporate more art, manipulatives, visuals, and music into their lessons. They tend to be more open to using Howard Gardner's multiple intelligences and other hands-on techniques. They tend to assign more group projects and activities and prefer a busy, active, noisy classroom environment. The classroom will typically have materials and books scattered all over.

Putting the Knowledge to Work in the Classroom

Researchers (Hardiman, 2003; Jensen, 1996) believe that both the left and right hemispheres need to be activated to enhance learning. For example, to teach algebra using both sides of the brain, you could use text and lecture presentation to help activate the left hemisphere and manipulatives, pictures, graphs, and other visual material to activate the right hemisphere. Activities such as cooperative learning may be brain-based if "it incorporates the intellect and the emotions and calls for spontaneous adaptations to meaningful, intellectually challenging issues" (Caine, Caine and Crowell, 1994, p. 9).

Incorporating left- and right-brain teaching strategies and learning activities can enrich students' learning—and it's manageable. Take a look at the following lesson (pages 50–52) designed for primary students to see how easily these ideas can be integrated into a lesson.

In the lesson, all students participate in the read-aloud and discussion, listen to the recording, and examine the sample of honeycomb. In small groups, students choose to conduct Internet research or read from other theme books about bees. Then the groups prepare a presentation about the information they've read or researched; there are presentations options that appeal to both left- and right-brained students. For the culminating activity, students create a bee from craft materials.

All students learn the content and meet the objectives, although the way they do it varies. All students must participate in left-brain and right-brain activities, so students can connect to the content through their strengths, but they also work with their less-developed side. The result is a dynamic lesson that all students can participate in and learn from. Table 4.1 on page 49 summarizes some ideas and suggestions to consider as you plan instruction to meet the needs of left- and right-brain students.

Table 4.1 Teaching Strategies for Left- and Right-Brain Learners

For Left-Brain Learners	For Right-Brain Learners
Provide a quiet, orderly space within the classroom, since left-brain learners often prefer this type of environment and need space to work independently. If your class is predominantly left-brained, consider placing desks in orderly rows.	Provide space for group work where students can collaborate in pairs or in small groups. If your class is predominantly right-brained, consider arranging desks in clusters.
Provide lots of light in the classroom.	Provide spaces with dimmed lighting.
Provide structure and clear directions to assignments.	Provide choices and incorporate hands-on activities such as role-play, experiments, and simulations.
Offer opportunities for students to work alone.	Offer opportunities for students to work in groups.
Allow students to problem solve by breaking down problems into parts and solving them in a step-by-step manner.	Allow students to problem solve by viewing problems holistically, making estimates, and using intuition.
Provide structured classroom and homework activities, such as choral reading, writing papers, and doing Internet research. These students often enjoy oral drills, such as spelling bees and reciting math facts.	Provide open-ended, hands-on classroom and homework activities, such as creating graphs, dioramas, and mobiles to demonstrate their learning.
Teach math through direct instruction: Explain the rules verbally and demonstrate how to solve problems step by step.	Teach math with manipulatives such as Cuisenaire Rods, fingers, blocks. Seeing and doing helps the right-brain student learn math.
Allow lots of time for reading. Left-brain students love to read, and they will remember the sequence of the story and the details. However, they may have trouble determining the main idea or making inferences. Think aloud for them, showing the steps you take to identify the main idea and make inferences.	Allow lots of time for reading. Right-brain students usually read to see the main idea or the big picture. They are typically good at summarizing, but have trouble remembering details. Use graphic organizers to help them remember and organize key details and ideas.
Offer opportunities for students to conduct Internet searches and Web quests.	Offer opportunities for students to use computer graphics and Web design.
Invite students to explore their brain preferences and have them write an outline and a paper that describes the results of their survey (see pages 43–44) and connects the findings to their life.	Invite students to explore their brain preferences (see survey on pages 43–44) and have them use magazine pictures and drawings to make a collage or a mobile to demonstrate who they are, their interests, and their goals.

Left-Brain / Right-Brain Lesson

Topic: *Bees*

Step 1: Establish Goals and Objectives

Goal: Integrate science and literature to build content-area knowledge and develop reading skills.

Science Objectives: To learn about insects, honeybees

1. *To identify the three main parts of the honeybee (the head, thorax, and abdomen) and their functions*
2. *To identify the three kinds of bees (worker bees, drones, and the queen bee) and their roles*
3. *To study the honeycomb and its uses to the bees (to make honey and to live) and to people (to make candles, chewing gum, lubricants)*

Reading Objectives: To develop comprehension skills

1. *Identify the main ideas in Bee Tree by Patricia Polacco read by teacher to class.*
2. *Read and respond to other books on topic; read individually by the student.*

Step 2: Choose Materials and Determine Lesson Structure

Materials

1. *Books: The Bee Tree, The Bee Man of Orn and Other Fanciful Tales, or Honey From My Heart for You, Friend*
2. *Recording of Rimsky-Korsakov's "Flight of the Bumblebee"*
3. *Honeycomb samples*
4. *Pattern of bee parts; art materials for culminating project (black pipe cleaners, buttons, and wax paper)*

Structure: Whole Group, Small Group, Choice Activities, Special Events, Etc.

Whole group reading and discussing main text; and related activities

Small group reading and research; group presentation

Step 3: Incorporate Left-Brain Activities (Whole Group, Small Group, Individual)

1. *Students listen to teacher read Patricia Polacco's book The Bee Tree.*
2. *Students and teacher discuss themes of the book; teacher models how to determine main idea.*

3. Students listen to teacher's explanation of bees and honeycombs.

4. Students write one to three paragraphs on the products that are made from honeycombs (crayons, waxed paper, chewing gum, earplugs, floor wax).

5. Students look up bee topics on the Internet; topics could be honeycombs, products made from honeycombs, the body of the honeybee, the honeybee colony, kinds of bees, beekeeping.

6. Groups of students read theme books such as The Bee Man of Orn and Other Fanciful Tales or Honey From My Heart for You, Friend. In small groups, they discuss books and connect to the read-aloud book and other information they've learned about the topic.

7. Students prepare a group presentation, using one of the following options:
(a) Present the plot of the book that the group read (b) Present Internet research

Step 4: Incorporate Right-Brain Activities (Whole Group, Small Group, Individual)

1. Students look at pictures as teacher reads The Bee Tree.

2. Students first listen quietly with their eyes closed to "bee music," Rimsky-Korsakov's "Flight of the Bumblebee."

3. Students then buzz around the classroom fast like bees to feel how fast bees move, buzzing in tune with the music in "Flight of the Bumblebee."

4. Students examine a real honeycomb to see how bees use some of the cells of the honeycomb to hold either eggs and baby bees, and other cells to store nectar and pollen.

5. Students eat part of the honeycomb and taste the sweetness of the natural bee honey spread onto a small sugar cookie.

6. Students go outdoors and search for likely spots for bee trees.

7. Each student makes a bee by cutting from the pattern of each of the three body parts (the head, thorax, and abdomen). Students can use black pipe cleaners for the antennae and six legs, two buttons for eyes, and wax paper for wings.

8. Small group: Students prepare a group presentation, using one of the following options—
(a) Make a poster depicting a major scene from the book they read (b) Role-play important scenes from the book

Step 5: Evaluate

Use a rubric to evaluate papers and presentation.
Give credit for participation in other activities.

Understanding Your Students

A large number of teachers have told me that they have benefited greatly from knowing their students' left-, right-, or middle-brain preference. They report that their students are fascinated to discover their own preference, and are thrilled when teachers provide assignments with choices on how to complete them. Students with strong left- or right-brain tendencies generally prefer to be taught to their neurological strengths. Although they can learn by different methods, they get most excited and involved when they can learn and do assignments in their area of strength. Lisa Sanford is a sixth-grade teacher in Lowell, Massachusetts, who frequently gives her students the choice to complete either a left-brain assignment or a right-brain assignment. Her students took a questionnaire, similar to the Alert Scale, at the beginning of the year when she taught them about their brain, and the differences in the left and right hemispheres. Lisa reports that her students love knowing about their brain preference. She has observed that the strong left-brain students typically select the left-brain assignment, and the strong right-brain students typically select the right-brain assignments to complete.

On pages 53–54 is a questionnaire that I designed for students in grades 1–8. As you give the questionnaire to your students, instruct them to circle the most appropriate answer for each of the 10 items. It's okay if you read the questions to them. When they are finished, help them tally the number of left-brain choices (L); right-brain choices (R); and middle-brain choices (M), and discuss the results. Since there are 12 questions, 6 or more in one area indicates a preference for that mode of learning. A score of 8 or more in one of the three areas indicates a strong preference for that mode.

There are various ways that teachers have incorporated information about hemisphere dominance into the school curriculum. Some teachers will integrate discussions of the left and right hemispheres into their science lessons, while others will incorporate the lessons via English/ language arts.

After taking the questionnaire, one fourth-grade teacher named Roger asked his students to write a paper on their left-, right-, or middle-brain strengths. He asked them to support the findings of the questionnaire by linking its results to their interests, hobbies, and preferred topics in school. Roger told me that the students maintained interest in this topic throughout the school year. One of his middle-brain students told him that, "I am going to work on strengthening my right brain by taking trumpet lessons!"

The Connell Left-/ Middle-/ Right-Brain Inventory for Childre

Choose the one phrase that best completes each sentence.

When I read, I usually find that I

_____ hear the words inside my head. (L)
X _____ see what I am reading in my mind. (R)
__✓__ both hear and see. (M)

When I am trying to give directions I usually

_____ explain how to get there. (L)
_____ draw a map. (R)
X __✓__ both draw a map and explain. (M)

When I am not at school, I would prefer to

_____ e-mail my friends. (L)
__✓__ play sports. (R)
X _____ e-mail or play sports. (M)

At school, I would prefer to do my work by

__✓__ drawing or painting. (R)
_____ writing. (L)
X _____ both drawing and writing. (M)

When trying to memorize words, it is easier for me to

X __✓__ sound them out and say them over and over. (L)
_____ remember when they were on the page. (R)
_____ use a combination of these techniques. (M)

I learn best from my teacher when she

_____ explains things clearly. (L)
__✓__ uses lots of pictures, graphs, and overheads. (R)
X _____ uses both words and pictures. (M)

As far as being on time goes, I

X _____ am almost always on time. (L)
_____ am often late. (R)
__✓__ am sometimes late and sometimes on time. (M)

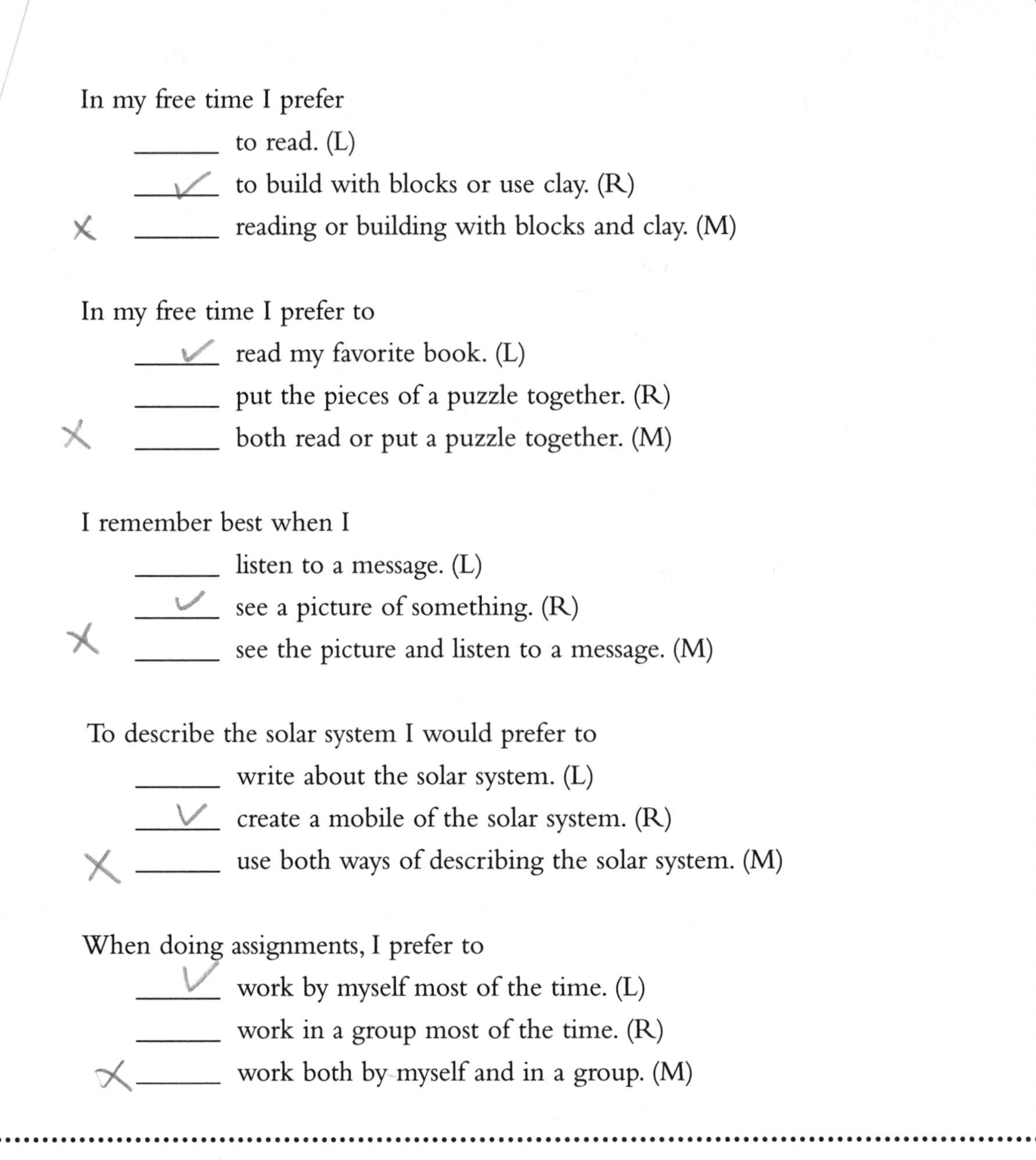

In my free time I prefer

______ to read. (L)

______ to build with blocks or use clay. (R)

______ reading or building with blocks and clay. (M)

In my free time I prefer to

______ read my favorite book. (L)

______ put the pieces of a puzzle together. (R)

______ both read or put a puzzle together. (M)

I remember best when I

______ listen to a message. (L)

______ see a picture of something. (R)

______ see the picture and listen to a message. (M)

To describe the solar system I would prefer to

______ write about the solar system. (L)

______ create a mobile of the solar system. (R)

______ use both ways of describing the solar system. (M)

When doing assignments, I prefer to

______ work by myself most of the time. (L)

______ work in a group most of the time. (R)

______ work both by myself and in a group. (M)

Scoring—Count up the number of responses you had for each L, R, and M.

______ = Ls (left-brain choices)

______ = Rs (right-brain choices)

______ = Ms (middle-brain choices)

6–8 circled in one area indicates a preference for that mode of learning.

9–12 circled in one area indicates a strong preference for that mode of learning.

Please remember that this questionnaire is "informal," and it does not necessarily provide a wholly accurate picture of which hemisphere is stronger. Remember, we all use both hemispheres when we learn and play.

Reaching Left-Brain and Right-Brain Students

Psychologists (Cherry, Godwin, and Staples, 1989) discuss the importance of setting up activities for each student to use his or her hemispheric strength in the classroom. They discuss providing each student with an opportunity to enrich the depth and breadth of his or her dominant hemisphere. These educators also stress that students will benefit from processing material in their less dominant hemisphere as well. Thus teachers would help students learn by creating different avenues to learn the same content (for example, lectures *and* group work). Let's revisit Dorothy and Sam from the opening of this chapter and explore how we might use our understanding of left-brain/right-brain preferences to support their learning.

A Sample Left-Brain Lesson for Dorothy

Imagine you have a student like Dorothy, who scores strong left on a left-brain preference test for children. Her right hemisphere is significantly weaker than her left; she has great difficulty understanding lessons with a visual-spatial orientation. Dorothy is a perfectionist. When the fourth-grade teacher initiates art lessons, Dorothy believes that she cannot do the work successfully. She is afraid to fail and consequently gets nauseous. Seeing the nurse accomplishes two things: It gets her away from an unpleasant situation and gives her time to regroup herself prior to reading.

What should you do?

First, you might explain to Dorothy that being a strong left-brain student, she is likely to excel in reading, writing, making outlines, rhyming, crossword puzzles, diagramming, and poetry, among other things. It is possible that she will not perform as well in art as she does in reading and writing. Tell her you will give her a book on how to make basic shapes so that she can improve upon and practice her sketching abilities.

As Dorothy's teacher, you can suggest activities to her or her parents that she is likely to be successful in and enjoy. After-school activities that left-brain students like Dorothy might enjoy include, but are not limited to, the following:

- Joining the debate team
- Writing for the school newspaper

- Participating in school government
- Writing the brochure for the school play
- Participating in individual sports such as martial arts, tennis, or swimming
- Writing stories, poems, essays
- Doing crossword puzzles

Let's say that you are introducing a unit on the solar system. Here are some left-brain teaching techniques that will help Dorothy and other strong-to-moderate left-brain students feel engaged and motivated during your lesson:

- Write an outline of the lesson on the board. Students with left-brain strengths appreciate sequence.
- Go ahead and lecture! These students love to listen to an expert and take notes.
- Discuss vocabulary words. Students like Dorothy often have a large vocabulary and are interested in words. Make a crossword puzzle on the solar system.
- Discuss the big concepts involved in the creation of the universe, how the solar system was formed, and so on. Left-brain students often like to think about and discuss abstract concepts.
- Assign individual assignments; students with left-brain preferences generally like to work alone.
- Ask students to write a paper on the solar system that includes both detail and conceptual analysis.
- Keep the room relatively quiet and orderly. Many students with left-brain strengths prefer not to hear other conversations when working on a stimulating project.

A Sample Right-Brain Lesson for Sam

Now, imagine you've got Sam in your class. Sam scores strong right on a brain-preference test for children. His left hemisphere is significantly weaker than his right and he has difficulty processing information presented orally. When the teacher lectures, or talks in compound, complex sentences, Sam gets anxious and overwhelmed and "shuts down." As he listens, the teacher's words run together, and the meaning becomes garbled.

His drawings comfort him; they are something he knows he can do well. Right-brain activities such as painting and drawing are activities that he can do easily and with pride.

What can you do to help Sam? First, as with Dorothy, you can explain the concept of hemispheric preference. You can tell Sam that he is a strong right-brain student. He is likely to excel in map reading, computer graphics, drawing, painting, model building, fixing things that are broken, and building with blocks and Legos. Perhaps his strength is not in listening to lectures or to conversations. Tell him that in order to help him learn the material, you will present numerous visual clues during your explanations, and that you will permit him to draw while you talk, as long as he is drawing about the topic the class is discussing.

As Sam's teacher, you can suggest activities to Sam and/or his parents that he is likely to both enjoy and be successful in. After-school activities that right-brained students like Sam might enjoy include, but are not limited to, the following:

- Playing group sports such as basketball, football, volleyball, or soccer
- Playing in the band, singing with the chorus, or taking voice lessons
- Joining the drama club or acting in the school play
- Designing scenery and/or costumes for the school play
- Joining the photography club or taking pictures for the yearbook
- Being a majorette
- Taking art lessons: ceramics, painting, sculpture
- Gardening
- Doing elaborate jigsaw puzzles

When introducing the lesson on the solar system, here are some right-brain teaching techniques that will help Sam, and other students with moderate to strong right-brain strengths, pay attention during your lesson:

- During the lecture, either write the main points on the board or pass out a study guide outline that students can fill in as you present orally. These visual clues will help students focus even though you are lecturing.
- Use the overhead, the whiteboard, or the chalkboard frequently. Since students are apt to miss the points discussed verbally, the visual pointers will help the students "see" the points and aid in overall comprehension.
- Make time for group activities during the solar system lesson.

Right-brain students tend to enjoy the company of others. Let students make projects in groups that use their visual-spatial right-brain strengths.

- Allow students to make a project, such as one with poster board, a mobile, a diorama, or papier-mâché planets of the solar system in lieu of writing a paper. Students like Sam are gifted at using their eye-hand coordination. These less conventional assignments still require that students learn the material.
- Play music such as "2001 Space Odyssey." Discuss how space might feel to an astronaut. Students with right-brain strengths are intuitive and like to "get in touch with their feelings" during the school day.
- Bring in charts and maps of the universe and let the students find the Milky Way. Maps and graphs make use of the students' strong right-brain, visual-spatial skills.

I believe that it is good practice to tell all students that we each have our own individual neurological strengths and weaknesses, that teachers do not expect everyone to be perfect in every area, that it is okay to make mistakes, and that it is great to ask for help.

You can reveal your own neurological strengths and weaknesses as an example. When you convey these messages to students, you will let them see that you are on their side. They will be grateful that you understand their learning style and are willing to assign projects and assignments in their area of strength throughout the year. Your students, especially those with strong left- or right-brain strengths, will be relieved to know it is okay not to get perfect scores in all of the very diverse areas that they encounter in school.

A Sample Unit Incorporating Left- and Right-Brain Strategies

You do not have to design entire lessons using only left- or right-brain activities. In fact, ideally, you can offer lessons that contain both left- and right-brain elements. The following is part of a large thematic unit on ancient Mesopotamia that I presented to a class of fourth-grade students. I planned the activities to include left-, right- and middle-brain learners in hopes of reaching all students. I followed a five-step planning process to ensure I met my academic goals and incorporated enough choices for left- and right-brain students. You'll find my planning template on page 64.

A Teaching Goal

I encourage you to set the following goal for yourself: If you are a left-brain teacher, try to incorporate at least one right-brain methodology (overheads, videos, music, role-playing, dance, or group projects) into your lessons; if you are a right-brain teacher, try adding more direct teaching, more speaking, or assigning more individual and/or research-oriented projects. If you are middle brain, please select and incorporate something new from either area. You'll see some sample goals set by teachers on the next page.

As you set your goals and review the various teaching strategies and learning activities presented in this chapter, consider this simple way to begin. When assigning a traditional project, such as a book report, offer options to students for how to complete the project. For a book report, you could allow the following options:

- Write the report using an outline.
- Present the report to the class from an outline.
- Draw and color a major scene from the book.
- Design and create a mobile, poster, or diorama.
- Dance a scene from the book.
- Write a poem and put it to music.
- Act out a particularly poignant scene.
- Create a different ending to the book.

It's fascinating to watch students gravitate toward their neurological strengths when given a choice of assignments. Those with moderate to strong right-brain strengths will choose to draw, act, or create. Those with the left-brain preference will choose to write or speak. In this way, you allow students to demonstrate their learning from their strengths. Students are learning the content as long as the options you give are academically rigorous and the students are engaged in the process.

Looking Ahead

The left-/right-/middle-brain perspective provides one brain-based avenue that we can use to get to know ourselves and our students. In the following chapter, we will examine ourselves and our students from the perspective of multiple intelligences.

Sample Left-Brain/Right-Brain/Middle-Brain Goals

I am a left-brain teacher during most of the day.
I like to talk and present exciting presentations to the students. I like them to get into discussions with me.

MY GOAL: In order to better engage my right-brain and middle-brain students, I will . . . *plan a hands-on project in both science and history during the next two months. Students will work on creating these projects in small groups.*

I am a right-brain teacher during most of the day.
I have students engaged in a multitude of exciting projects.

MY GOAL: In order to better engage my left-brain and middle-brain students, I will . . . *present material orally three days a week.*

I am a middle-brain teacher and am already reasonably flexible.
I am already pretty flexible, however, I see that I tug to the left.

MY GOAL: To expand my teaching repertoire, I will . . . *incorporate more right-brain methodologies into my lessons, including use of the overhead and poster presentations..*

Your Left-Brain/Right-Brain/Middle-Brain Goals

Please fill in one of these boxes.

I am a left-brain teacher during most of the day.

MY GOAL: In order to better engage my right-brain and middle-brain students, I will . . .

I am a right-brain teacher during most of the day.

MY GOAL: In order to better engage my left-brain and middle-brain students, I will . . .

I am a middle-brain teacher and am already reasonably flexible.

MY GOAL: To expand my teaching repertoire, I will . . .

Left-Brain / Right-Brain Lesson

Topic: *Ancient Mesopotamia*

Step 1: Establish Goals and Objectives

1. *To make aspects of ancient history come alive to the students.*
2. *To help students understand life on Earth as it was 5,000 years ago.*
3. *To contrast life on Earth today with the time of the ancient civilization of Mesopotamia.*
4. *To incorporate and enhance individual writing skills.*

Step 2: Choose Materials and Determine Lesson Structure

Materials

1. *Books: Gilgamesh the King, The Revenge of Ishtar, and The Last Quest of Gilgamesh*
2. *Recordings: soundtrack of Aida*
3. *Food samples: pomegranates, apricots, dates, figs, plums as well as fruit-sandwich cookies made with apricots*
4. *Clay tablets and stylus*

Structure: Whole Group, Small Group, Choice Activities, Special Events, Etc.

whole class

Step 3: Incorporate Left-Brain Activities (Whole Group, Small Group, Individual)

1. *A discussion of the four main characters prior to reading storybooks (Gilgamesh, Enkidu, Shamhat and her harp, Ishtar)*
2. *Reading three storybooks (Gilgamesh the King, The Revenge of Ishtar, and The Last Quest of Gilgamesh) with discussion*
3. *A discussion of new concepts and vocabulary words (immortality, abyss, quest)*

   Thought-provoking questions (for example, why did Gilgamesh want to destroy death and achieve immortality? Would you want to live forever? Did Gilgamesh achieve immortality? How did Shamhat's harp music "tame" Enkidu? What spirits do Shamhat and Ishtar represent in the trilogy? What does the lion in the last book represent?)
4. *A lesson contrasting life in ancient Mesopotamia with our lives today*

(a) Compare and contrast life for boys and girls today with that of the boys and girls in Mesopotamia. Include both an individual writing activity and a group discussion.

(b) An examination of different expectations for girls and boys in terms of school and work

(c) A written three- to four-page paper on this topic with a rubric included for writing expectations

Step 4: Incorporate Right-Brain Activities (Whole Group, Small Group, Individual)

1. Playing harp (lyre) music. I asked the students, "What is this special instrument that is over 5,000 years old? What is the message in this music? Can you see how Shamhat could use it to conquer Enkidu?"

   (a) I played two selections from Elton John and Tim Rice's Aida. (In addition, the story of Aida was discussed from a historical perspective of ancient Egypt).

   (b) Students moved and danced to the music; they were asked to describe how the harp music made them feel.

2. Showing the illustrations in the three storybooks as I read.

3. Bringing in a timeline in order to see "the whole perspective." I then asked questions: "Can you imagine the world 5,000 years ago? Do you find it interesting that people are still similar after this length of time?" (Notice that this doubles as a right- and a left-brain activity—the left aspect is the sequence of time, the right aspect is the whole picture of time.)

4. Bringing in a globe and map to show that ancient Mesopotamia was located where Syria and Iraq are today near the Mediterranean Sea, and near the Tigris and Euphrates Rivers.

5. Comparing foods today with those 5,000 years ago.

   (a) Lectured and discussed farming vs. food industry, and eating locally only vs. eating imported food.

   (b) We sampled food brought in "from ancient Mesopotamia," including pomegranates, apricots, dates, figs, and plums, as well as fruit-sandwich cookies made with apricots. Students chose what to sample.

6. Writing in cuneiform.

   (a) Cuneiform writing constitutes one of the first written number systems to exist. The fourth-grade students were shown the five cuneiform symbols. They worked some subtraction problems by translating the symbols into numbers.

   (b) The students were given clay tablets and a stylus to write their names.

7. Displaying my scarab jewelry, an ancient Egyptian symbol of resurrection and eternal life. The students looked up the symbols on my scarab bracelet and earrings.

Step 5: Evaluate

Use a rubric to evaluate student contributions to discussion and the compare/contrast paper. Give credit for participation in the cuneiform writing activities.

Left-Brain / Right-Brain Lesson Planning Template

Topic:

Step 1: **Establish Goals and Objectives**

Step 2: **Choose Materials and Determine Lesson Structure**

Materials

Structure: Whole Group, Small Group, Choice Activities, Special Events, Etc.

Step 3: **Incorporate Left-Brain Activities**
(Whole Group, Small Group, Individual)

Step 4: **Incorporate Right-Brain Activities**
(Whole Group, Small Group, Individual)

Step 5: **Evaluate**

Chapter 5

What Are Multiple Intelligences?

"Brain research establishes and confirms that multiple complex and concrete experiences are essential for meaningful learning and teaching."

—Renate Caine and Geoffrey Caine (1994, p. 5)

Howard Gardner's theory of multiple intelligence offers an exciting avenue on our ongoing "Who Am I?" spiral path. It provides us with keen insights into our own neurological strengths and weaknesses. In addition, the theory of multiple intelligences provides us with a multitude of new ways to teach our students.

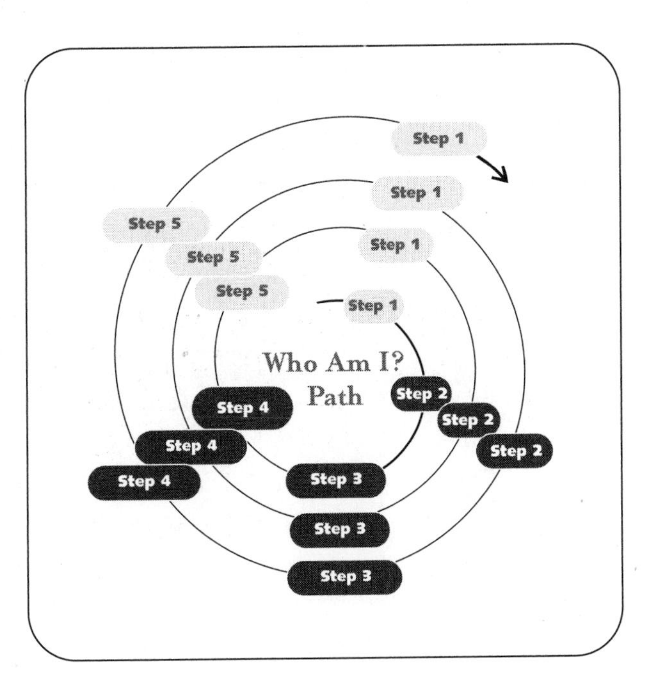

The Theory of Multiple Intelligences

The theory of multiple intelligences is making a tremendous impact in the field of education. Gone are the days when we believed that students should be smart only in the reading and math areas. Now we recognize that there are many different kinds of intelligence. Even the ways in which we test students have changed; Marge Scherer (1997) explains, "Some standardized tests today require writing samples, interpretations of charts, and drawings, allowing students to display their intelligence in a variety of ways" (p.7).

Research has demonstrated that the multiple intelligences work independently of one another. In terms of brain-based learning, what is especially significant is that the intelligences have a physiological location in the brain (Gardner, 1983). Drawing upon neuropsychological research, Gardner suggests that when "the appropriate observational lenses are donned, the peculiar nature of each intelligence emerges with sufficient (and often surprising) clarity" (p. 9). For example, when we use our verbal-linguistic intelligence via reading, writing, or speaking, there is increased brain activity in our left temporal lobe. When we use our visual-spatial intelligence to color, draw, or sculpt with clay, there is increased brain activity in our right occipital lobe.

Depending on how you interpret it, Gardner's theory recognizes either eight and a half, or nine different human intelligences. The original seven intelligences described in Gardner's *Frames of Mind* include the verbal-linguistic, logical-mathematical, bodily-kinesthetic, spatial, musical, interpersonal, and intrapersonal (Gardner, 1983). In 1997, Gardner added an eighth intelligence: naturalistic. The most recent addition is the existential intelligence, which Gardner credits as a "half intelligence," because he has not been able to find a physiological location for it in the brain (Gardner 1998, 1999). Thomas Armstrong (2000) explains existential intelligence as "any rendering of the spectrum of human intelligences that addresses humanity's long-standing efforts to come to grips with the ultimate questions of life: 'Who are we?' 'What's it all about?' 'Why is there evil?' 'Where is humanity heading?' 'Is there meaning in life?' and so forth" (p. 127). For the purpose of this book, I will elevate the existential intelligence to a full intelligence, making it our ninth intelligence.

Table 5.1 describes each intelligence. It also discusses likely career paths of people who have strengths in the individual areas.

Table 5.1 Overview of Multiple Intelligences

	Description	Characteristics of People Strongly Developed in This Intelligence	Preferred Careers of People With This Intelligence
	Verbal-Linguistic. This intelligence covers a continuum, with speaking strengths on one end and writing strengths on the other end. People with this intelligence can excel on one or the other or both ends of the continuum.	Verbal-linguistic people love words. Words are their primary way of thinking and solving problems. They tend to have excellent auditory receptive (input) skills and verbal expressive (output) skills. They use words to persuade, argue, entertain, or teach. These people are good writers, speakers, or both.	teachers, principals, storytellers, TV talk show hosts, journalists, newspaper editors, writers, poets, and authors
47 ×8	**Logical-Mathematical.** This intelligence also covers a continuum, with mathematics on one end and science and research on the other.	Logical-mathematical people love numbers. They can easily interpret data and analyze abstract patterns. They have a well-developed ability to reason and are good at chess and computer programming. They think in terms of causes and effects.	math teachers, special education teachers, tax accountants, mathematicians, statisticians, scientists, doctors, and medical researchers
	Spatial. This intelligence encompasses the eye-hand skills. These people can see images in their mind's eye and replicate this image with paint, sculpture, architectural blueprints, and buildings.	Spatial people think and process information in pictures and images. They have excellent visual receptive skills and excellent fine motor skills. People with this intelligence use their eyes and hands to create wonderful products. They can build with Legos, read maps, and put together 1,000-piece jigsaw puzzles.	architects, artists, sculptors, interior decorators, seamstresses, beauticians, book illustrators, cartoonists, carpenters, art teachers, vocational teachers, car designers, clothes designers, and mechanics
	Musical. This intelligence includes those who compose and those who perform music. Gardner believes that we need to bring this intelligence into our classroom more.	Musical people think, feel, and process information primarily through sound. They have a superior ability to perceive, compose, and/or perform music. Musically smart people constantly hear musical tones in their head; they think and feel music. Music connects directly to our emotions in the limbic system and can be used to enhance memory.	musicians, songwriters, music teachers, sound engineers, composers, and conductors
	Bodily-Kinesthetic. This intelligence includes a wide spectrum of physical abilities that range from athletics to dance, swimming, acting, gymnastics, and the martial arts.	Bodily-kinesthetic people are highly aware of the world through touch and movement. There is a special harmony between their body and their mind. They can control their body with grace and expertise. They are aware of their gut feelings. Those with this intelligence engage in group sports, dance, cheerleading, swimming, gymnastics, and martial arts.	ballet dancers, actors, professional athletes, physical therapists, occupational therapists, coaches, physical education teachers, dance teachers, and mime artists

...ble 5.1 Overview of Multiple Intelligences *continued*

	Description	Characteristics of People Strongly Developed in This Intelligence	Preferred Careers of People With This Intelligence
	Interpersonal. This intelligence refers to the ability to get along with others. They are effective leaders, communicators, and mediators.	Interpersonal people have a strong ability to get along with others, to interact and relate effectively. They are good leaders. They use their insights about others to negotiate, persuade, and obtain information. They like to interact with others and usually have lots of friends. They often select their mentors.	political leaders, religious leaders, teachers, principals, nurses, TV and radio talk show hosts, bartenders, salespeople, psychologists
	Intrapersonal. This refers to an individual's ability to recognize and accept his or her own strengths and weaknesses. People with a strong intrapersonal intelligence have a deep awareness of their feelings, ideas, and goals. Many believe that this is the most important intelligence to develop.	Intrapersonal people have a strong ability to know themselves. They know, and accept, their strong, moderate, and weak multiple intelligences. They are able to assume responsibility for their actions and feelings. They have keen intuition and inner wisdom. At an emotional level, they are able to engage in deep introspective thoughts; they have a deep awareness of their inner feelings, ideas, and dreams. People with this intelligence need a lot time alone to process and create.	clergy persons, theologians, writers, entrepreneurs, inventors, teachers, psychologists, and researchers
	Naturalistic. This intelligence refers to an individual's natural interest in the environment. People with strong naturalistic intelligence easily recognize and categorize plants, animals, and rocks.	Naturalistic people have a deep interest in the environment. They like to be in nature and they want to protect it from pollution. They can navigate easily in the natural world. They see the patterns in nature, recognizing the different flora, fauna, rocks, and birds. As teachers they bring nature into the classroom and their students outside with more regularity than teachers who are not strong in this intelligence.	science teachers, Girl or Boy Scout leaders, ecologists, environmentalists, water quality monitors, marine biologists, and meteorologists
	Existential. This is the intelligence that Gardner refers to as a "half intelligence" because he could not find a physiological location for it in the brain. I also call this a spiritual intelligence, as those who score high in this intelligence are concerned with life's big questions.	Existentialists are those concerned, often at an early age, with the big, piercing questions: Who am I? Why do we die? What is the meaning of life? I believe that existential intelligence overlaps or coincides with a spiritual awareness and concern for humankind.	philosophers, priests, rabbis, or ministers; history and philosophy teachers; and inspirational speakers or writers

Discovering Your Multiple Intelligences

The first piece of good news is that we each possess all nine of the intelligences. Gardner (1983) believes that most of us have several highly developed intelligences, a few moderately developed intelligences, and the rest remain underdeveloped. The second piece of good news is that psychologist and educator Thomas Armstrong (1994, 2000, 2003) believes that with a combination of encouragement, enrichment, and good instruction, we can enhance our strongest intelligences, as well as develop our moderate and underdeveloped intelligences. In *You're Smarter Than You Think: A Kid's Guide to Multiple Intelligences* (2003), Armstrong affirms that students can continue to develop each of their intelligences. He states, "No matter what kind of ability you have in a given [intelligence], you can explore, grow, and develop it. Whether you have trouble spelling 'dictionary' or you're a future best-selling author, you can become more word smart" (p. 5). For each intelligence, Armstrong lists 10 fun ways for students to become more developed in that intelligence. For example, some of his suggestions to become more nature smart include: study the sky on a clear night; learn the constellations; go bird-watching with binoculars and a guidebook; start a garden; watch nature shows on television; or read books and magazines about nature.

The same principle applies to adults; our brains are continually making new neural connections. As an adult, I find it reassuring to know that we can continue to develop our intelligences as we age. My husband, Jim, took piano lessons for the first time at age 39. Even at that ripe old age, he was able to learn to play the piano well. Jim's brain changed because of his experience with music, his temporal lobes were enhanced. James Zull (2002) states, "The knowledge in our minds consists of neural networks in our brains, so if that knowledge is to grow, the neural networks must physically change" (p. 112). In the case of my husband, his dedicated practice and repetition helped him form new, strong neural networks. Zull confirms, "Neurons that are repeatedly used grow stronger synapses and more effective neural networks. And the more they fire, the more they send out new branches looking for more new and useful connections" (p. 117). Zull also connects this brain-based learning to students—"surprising as it may sound, there are ways that a teacher can encourage all these types of change in the synapses of her students" (p.112).

Multiple Intelligences Survey

Put a check next to each sentence that describes you. Tally your checks at the end of each section and calculate the score.

Section 1

____ I enjoy categorizing things by common traits.
____ Ecological issues are important to me.
____ Hiking and camping are enjoyable activities.
____ I enjoy working on a garden.
____ I believe preserving our national parks is important.
____ Putting things in hierarchies makes sense to me.
____ Animals are important in my life.
____ My home has a recycling system in place.
____ I enjoy studying biology, botany and/or zoology.
____ I spend a great deal of time outdoors.
____ **TOTAL for Section 1**
____ **Score for Section 1 = Total x 10**

Section 2

____ I easily pick up on patterns.
____ I focus in on noise and sounds.
____ Moving to a beat is easy for me.
____ I've always been interested in playing an instrument.
____ The cadence of poetry intrigues me.
____ I remember things by putting them in a rhyme.
____ Concentration is difficult while listening to a radio or television.
____ I enjoy many kinds of music.
____ Musicals are more interesting than dramatic plays.
____ Remembering song lyrics is easy for me.
____ **TOTAL for Section 2**
____ **Score for Section 2 = Total x 10**

Section 3

____ I keep my things neat and orderly.
____ Step-by-step directions are a big help.
____ Solving problems comes easily to me.
____ I get easily frustrated with disorganized people.
____ I can complete calculations quickly in my head.
____ Puzzles requiring reasoning are fun.
____ I can't begin an assignment until all my questions are answered.
____ Structure helps me be successful.
____ I find working on a computer spreadsheet or database rewarding.
____ Things have to make sense to me or I am dissatisfied.
____ **TOTAL for Section 3**
____ **Score for Section 3 = Total x 10**

Section 4

____ It is important to see my role in the "big picture" of things.
____ I enjoy discussing questions about life.
____ Religion is important to me.
____ I enjoy viewing art masterpieces.
____ Relaxation and meditation exercises are rewarding.
____ I like visiting breathtaking sites in nature.
____ I enjoy reading ancient and modern philosophers.
____ Learning new things is easier when I understand their value.
____ I wonder if there are other forms of intelligent life in the universe.
____ Studying history and ancient culture helps give me perspective.
____ **TOTAL for Section 4**
____ **Score for Section 4 = Total x 10**

Section 5

____ I learn best interacting with others.
____ The more the merrier.
____ Study groups are very productive for me.
____ I enjoy chat rooms.
____ Participating in politics is important.
____ Television and radio talk shows are enjoyable.
____ I am a "team player."
____ I dislike working alone.
____ Clubs and extracurricular activities are fun.
____ I pay attention to social issues and causes.
____ **TOTAL for Section 5**
____ **Score for Section 5 = Total x 10**

Section 6

____ I enjoy making things with my hands.
____ Sitting still for long periods of time is difficult for me.
____ I enjoy outdoor games and sports.
____ I value nonverbal communication such as sign language.
____ A fit body is important for a fit mind.
____ Arts and crafts are enjoyable pastimes.
____ Expression through dance is beautiful.
____ I like working with tools.
____ I live an active lifestyle.
____ I learn by doing.
____ **TOTAL for Section 6**
____ **Score for Section 6 = Total x 10**

Source: ©*1999 Walter McKenzie,* Creative Classroom Consulting. *Reprinted by Permission*

Section 7

____ I enjoy reading all kinds of materials.

____ Taking notes helps me remember and understand.

____ I faithfully contact friends through letters and/or e-mail.

____ It is easy for me to explain my ideas to others.

____ I keep a journal.

____ Word puzzles like crosswords and jumbles are fun.

____ I write for pleasure.

____ I enjoy playing with words like puns, anagrams and spoonerisms.

____ Foreign languages interest me.

____ Debates and public speaking are activities I like to participate in.

____ **TOTAL for Section 2**

____ **Score for Section 2 = Total x 10**

Section 8

____ I am keenly aware of my moral beliefs.

____ I learn best when I have an emotional attachment to the subject.

____ Fairness is important to me.

____ My attitude affects how I learn.

____ Social justice issues concern me.

____ Working alone can be just as productive as working in a group.

____ I need to know why I should do something before I agree to do it.

____ When I believe in something I will give 100 percent effort to it

____ I like to be involved in causes that help others.

____ I am willing to protest or sign a petition to right a wrong.

____ **TOTAL for Section 8**

____ **Score for Section 8 = Total x 10**

Section 9

____ I can imagine ideas in my mind.

____ Rearranging a room is fun for me.

____ I enjoy creating art using varied media.

____ I remember well using graphic organizers.

____ Performance art can be very gratifying.

____ Spreadsheets are great for making charts, graphs and tables.

____ Three-dimensional puzzles bring me much enjoyment.

____ Music videos are very stimulating.

____ I can recall things in mental pictures.

____ I am good at reading maps and blueprints.

____ **TOTAL for Section 9**

____ **Score for Section 9 = Total x 10**

Source: ©1999 *Walter McKenzie,* Creative Classroom Consulting. *Reprinted by Permission*

Analysis of Multiple Intelligence Test and Observational Chart

Scoring—Fill in the chart below to highlight your strongest (scores of 60 to 100), moderate (scores of 50 to 40), and underdeveloped (scores of 30 to 0) intelligences.

60 40 Section 1 = Naturalistic Intelligence

70 30 Section 2 = Musical Intelligence

50 50 Section 3 = Logical-Mathematic Intelligence

60 50 Section 4 = Existential Intelligence

50 50 Section 5 = Interpersonal Intelligence

100 40 Section 6 = Bodily-Kinesthetic Intelligence

* 20 70 Section 7 = Verbal-Linguistic Intelligence

* 90 90 Section 8 = Intrapersonal Intelligence

80 50 Section 9 = Spatial Intelligence

Note: This is not a test. It is a snapshot in time of an individual's perceived multiple intelligence preferences.

My strongest multiple intelligences are (score 60–100):

verbal-Linguistic, intrapersonal

My moderate multiple intelligences are (score 50–40):

spatial, interpersonal, existential, naturalistic
bodily-Kinesthetic

My underdeveloped multiple intelligences are (score 30–0):

musical

Bruce Campbell is an educator and a writer who has extensive experience teaching and writing using the multiple intelligences (1996, 1989). He has applied Gardner's multiple intelligence theory to his third-, fourth-, and fifth-grade, multiage classroom for many years. In particular, he created multiple intelligence centers for his third-grade students. Each center was dedicated to one of Gardner's seven original intelligences (at the time, information regarding the naturalistic and existential intelligences had not been published). The physical structure of the classroom was arranged to accommodate the seven learning centers. Campbell planned his lessons so that any topic he presented to his students was taught in seven different ways using seven centers. The students spent about 20 minutes completing activities in each center; they moved in groups of three or four completing activities in all seven centers.

Campbell (1989) writes that teaching in the multiple intelligence way has also enhanced his learning: "I think my own seven intelligences are beginning to awaken to the challenge." It is exciting that as we teach intentionally using all of the intelligences, we also enhance the centers in our brain as well. In addition, we are also helping our students to develop their intelligences and to establish new neural networks!

Walter McKenzie developed the multiple intelligences survey in 1999–2000. Please take the time now to take the survey (pages 70–73) and score the results, as it will be beneficial for you to know which areas constitute your strongest, moderate, and underdeveloped multiple intelligences. Please complete each section by placing a "1" next to each statement you feel accurately describes you, then total the column in each section.

Multiple Intelligences That Work Together

Gardner has noted that although the intelligences are relatively independent of one another, they can be "fashioned and combined in a multiplicity of adaptive ways by individuals and cultures" (pp. 8-9). Gardner states that the intelligences "typically work in harmony" in individuals (p. 9). Looking at the intelligences involved in a Broadway musical, for example, we can see that in order to perform successfully, the actors must use a combination of their verbal-linguistic, bodily-kinesthetic, and musical intelligences.

What are the intelligences at work in creating a large vegetable garden? We would need to use a combination of spatial, intrapersonal, and logical-mathematical intelligences to plan where the vegetables will be planted. Additionally, bodily-kinesthetic and naturalistic intelligences would be used to physically sow seeds and to weed. In some individuals, an existential intelligence might come into play when they walk among the sprouting vegetables, fruits, and flowers.

In the classroom, teachers can construct lessons that use particular "blends" of the intelligences. When teachers consciously use the different intelligences in the classroom, they enrich the content, making it more accessible to learners. Let's revisit Renate and Geoffrey Caine's assertion: "Brain research establishes and confirms that multiple complex and concrete experiences are essential for meaningful learning and teaching" (1994, p. 5). Given this, we can see that using a combination of intelligences in any lesson will reinforce the concept we are teaching.

For example, when teaching students how to write the letters of the alphabet we can use a blend of intelligences. Instead of only demonstrating letter formation on the chalkboard and then having students use paper and pencil to write the letters themselves, we can also have students shape letters out of clay or wax sticks (spatial intelligence) and cut out sandpaper letters and feel them with their fingers (bodily-kinesthetic and spatial intelligences). We can turn on music and help them use their bodies to form the letters (musical and tactile kinesthetic intelligences). And to utilize the logical-mathematical intelligence, we can point out to students that there are only five vowels but 21 consonants in the alphabet. For more variety, we can let students work on the letters in pairs or small groups, thereby using the interpersonal intelligence as well.

When we help our students make academic connections using different intelligences, we are also helping one part of their brain link to other parts. Using multiple intelligences that work together helps to connect and strengthen neural pathways in the brain.

Connecting Multiple Intelligences and Left- and Right-Brain Strengths

There is a clear correlation between our hemispheric dominance (see Chapter Four) and which intelligences we are strongest in. The following chart makes a connection between our brain preference and our strongest intelligences.

You probably noticed that the naturalistic intelligence was specified under both left- and right-brain dominance. I think that it may depend on how you enjoy nature: would you rather enjoy nature by yourself, or with others? Do you like to garden, walk, or hike on your own? Do you like to walk alone by the ocean? Or do you like to enjoy nature with others, by being a Girl or Boy Scout leader or a camp counselor? Perhaps you signed up to take a night class in astronomy or a group canoe trip down the river.

Correlating Brain Dominance and Intelligences

Brain Dominance	Likely Strongest Intelligence
Left Brain	Verbal-Linguistic, Logical-Mathematical, Existential, Naturalistic, Intrapersonal
Right Brain	Spatial, Musical, Bodily-Kinesthetic, Naturalistic, Interpersonal
Middle Brain	A unique mixture of intelligences. Some people "tug" to the left, some to the right

Implications of Multiple Intelligence Theory for Teachers

Once we discover which of our own intelligences are well developed, we often become aware of our tendency to rely on our stronger and moderate intelligences when we teach. The corollary is that we rarely incorporate our weaker intelligences into our lesson plans, which is unfortunate for our students who are well developed in those particular intelligences. The rule is simple: The more intelligences we can incorporate into our lessons, the more students we will reach and connect to in an in-depth way. Even though it may feel unnatural at first, it is well worth the effort to incorporate learning activities that allow students with different intelligences to shine. The lists on pages 77–79 suggest materials and activities that appeal to students well developed in a particular intelligence; use them to spark ideas for integrating a variety of activities into your teaching.

In linking two concepts—brain hemisphere preference and multiple intelligences—we are also connecting existing neural passageways in the brain. In essence, this chapter is connecting new knowledge about multiple intelligences to prior knowledge about brain style. This is exactly what the research in brain-based learning suggests we do with students.

Verbal-Linguistic Intelligence

Materials

Students strong in verbal-linguistic intelligence will often enjoy working with the following materials:

- magazines, comic books, books
- paper, pens, pencils, colored pens
- computers and a printer

Activities

Students strong in verbal-linguistic intelligence will often enjoy the following activities:

- Completing crossword puzzles with their vocabulary words
- Playing games like Scrabble or Scrabble Junior
- Writing short descriptions of fun activities for a classroom newsletter
- Writing features articles for the school newspaper
- Writing letters to the editor in response to articles
- Writing to state representatives about local issues
- Using computer software such as:
  - a. electronic libraries (such as *World Library*)
  - b. desktop publishing (such as *Publish It!*)
  - c. word games (such as Missing Links)
  - d. word processing programs (such as Word)
- Creating poems for a class poetry book
- Entering their original poems in a poetry contest
- Listening to a storyteller
- Studying the habits of good speakers
- Telling a story to the class
- Participating in debates

Logical-Mathematical Intelligence

Materials

Students strong in logical-mathematical intelligence will often enjoy working with the following materials:

- calculators, math manipulatives, tangrams rulers, protractors, tape measures
- science books and workbooks, math books and workbooks
- computers

Activities

Students strong in logical-mathematical intelligence will often enjoy the following activities:

- Playing math games like dominoes, chess, checkers, and Monopoly
- Searching for patterns in the class-room, school, outdoors, and home
- Conducting experiments to demonstrate science concepts
- Using math and science software, such as Math Blaster, which reinforces math skills; King's Rule, a logic game
- Using Science Tool Kits for science programs
- Designing alphabetic or numeric codes
- Making up analogies

Spatial Intelligence

Materials

Students strong in spatial intelligence will often enjoy working with the following materials:

- colored paper, doodle books, and pens
- paints and paint brushes
- a variety of writing implements
- modeling clay
- puppets, puppet clothes, and props
- puzzles and Legos
- globes and maps
- digital and regular cameras

Activities

Students strong in spatial intelligence will often enjoy the following activities:

- Taking photographs for assignments and classroom newsletters
- Taking photographs for the school yearbook, school newsletter, or science assignments
- Using clay or play dough to make objects or represent concepts from content-area lessons
- Using pictorial models such as flow charts, visual maps, Venn diagrams, and timelines to connect new material to known information
- Taking notes using concept mapping, mind mapping, and clustering
- Using puppets to act out and reinforce concepts learned in class
- Using maps to study geographical locations discussed in class
- Illustrating poems for the class poetry book by drawing or using computer software
- Using software such as Dactyl Nightmare, a virtual-reality system software

Musical Intelligence

Materials

Students strong in musical intelligence will often enjoy working with the following materials:

- CD players and CDs, tape recorders and tapes
- musical instruments and sheet music

Activities

Students strong in musical intelligence will often enjoy the following activities:

- Writing their own songs and music about content-area topics
- Putting original poems to music, and then performing them for the class
- Incorporating a poem they have written with a melody they already know
- Listening to music from different historical periods
- Tape recording a poem over "appropriate" background music (soft music if describing a kitten, loud music if they are mad about pollution)
- Using rhythm and clapping to memorize math facts and other content-area information
- Listening to CDs that teach concepts like the alphabet, parts of speech, states and capitols. *School House Rocks* is ideal for elementary-aged students.

Interpersonal Intelligence

Materials

Students strong in interpersonal intelligence will often enjoy working with the following materials:

- Board games, cards

Activities

Students strong in interpersonal intelligence will often enjoy the following activities:

- Working in cooperative groups to design and complete projects
- Working in pairs to learn math facts
- Interviewing people with knowledge about content-area topics (such as a shopkeeper when studying economics)
- Tutoring younger students or classmates
- Using puppets to put on a puppet show

Bodily-Kinesthetic Intelligence

Materials

Students strong in bodily-kinesthetic intelligence will often enjoy working with the following materials:

- beanbags, blocks, woodworking materials
- sewing supplies, such as needle and thread, fabric
- books on athletics, clowns, dancers, actors, actresses, martial arts

Activities

Students strong in bodily-kinesthetic intelligence will often enjoy the following activities:

- Creating costumes for role-playing, skits, or simulations
- Performing skits, acting out scenes from books or key historical events
- Designing props for plays and skits
- Playing games like Twister and Simon Says
- Using charades to act out characters in a book, vocabulary words, animals, or other content-area topics
- Participating in scavenger hunts, searching for items related to a theme or unit
- Acting out concepts. For example, for the solar system "student planets" circle around a "student sun." Students line up appropriately to demonstrate events in a history timeline. Students act out punctuation marks (scratch their heads for question marks, jump up and down for an exclamation mark, sit for a period)
- Participating in "movement breaks" during the day; students perform Brain Gym exercises (see page 37); yoga, dance, or stretching exercises
- Building objects using blocks, cubes, or Legos to represent concepts from content-area lessons.
- Using software such as *Flight Simulator*, a motion-simulation game or LEGO to LOGO, hands-on construction kits that interface with computers

Intrapersonal Intelligence

Materials

Students strong in intrapersonal intelligence will often enjoy working with the following materials:

- motivational and inspirational books
- computers, paper, pencils

Activities

Students strong in intrapersonal intelligence will often enjoy the following activities:

- Writing reflective papers on content-area topics
- Writing essays from the perspective of historical figures, such as Civil War soldiers or suffragettes
- Writing a literary autobiography, reflecting on their reading life
- Writing goals for the future and planning ways to achieve them
- Using a software that allows them to work alone, such as *Decisions, Decisions*, a personal choice software; or the *Perfect Career*, career choice software
- Keeping journals or logs throughout the year
- Making a scrapbook for their poems, papers, and reflections

Naturalistic Intelligence

Materials

Students strong in naturalistic intelligence will often enjoy working with the following materials:

- environmental books and activities
- books on national parks
- books about plants, bugs, and small pets
- microscopes, magnifying glasses
- plants and pet supplies

Activities

Students strong in naturalistic intelligence will often enjoy the following activities:

- Caring for classroom plants
- Caring for classroom pets. Consider housing insects such as crickets and beetles if traditional pets are not feasible
- Sorting and classifying natural objects, such as rocks and leaves
- Researching animal habitats
- Observing natural surroundings

Existential Intelligence

Materials

Students strong in existential intelligence will often enjoy working with the following materials:

- books by philosophers and existentialists
- computers, paper, pens

Activities

Students strong in existential intelligence will often enjoy the following activities:

- Taking "thinking walks" and writing about the forces that they see in nature
- Writing reflective essays on topics from the content areas. For example, when studying the Civil War, students write "if you were Abraham Lincoln, what would you have been feeling when you were trying to decide whether or not to declare war on the South?"
- Discussing social issues; presenting ideas to the class
- Writing essays on social issues
- Conducting research on local issues
- Interviewing local politicians
- Responding to letters to the editor that appear in the local paper

Teaching Using Your Multiple Intelligences

This next exercise provides an opportunity for you to observe yourself as you teach. Which multiple intelligences do you use most often? Which ones aren't used at all? If you teach different classes on different days of the week, it would be beneficial to observe yourself in each of the classes.

Below is a hypothetical example of a typical fourth-grade teacher observing her use of multiple intelligences throughout the day. Following this is a blank observation page for you to fill in as you go about your day. The form can be photocopied and used multiple times; some teachers have filled in the form every day for a week in order to ascertain which intelligences they use most often, and which ones they use infrequently. Remember, incorporating the multiple intelligences that you use least often will help you reach more students, especially those who have been hard to reach!

Sample of Multiple Intelligences Teaching Observations During the Day

Time	**Class Taught**	**Description of Activity and/or Materials Used**	**Multiple Intelligence(s) Used by Teacher**
8:00–8:30	Friday Spelling Quiz	I dictated spelling quiz to class. Asked class to write two paragraphs using all of the words.	1. Verbal-Linguistic
8:30–9:15	Math Time	I used chalkboard to review homework assignment on multiplication. Had students work on problems individually.	1. Verbal-Linguistic (explanation) 2. Spatial (chalkboard) 3. Logical-Mathematical 4. Intrapersonal
9:15–11:00	History of China	I lectured on Chinese culture. I brought in some Chinese music and food for the class to try. Small groups from 9:45 to 10:15 working on a PowerPoint Presentation.	1. Verbal-Linguistic (explanation) 2. Musical 3. Bodily-Kinesthetic 4. Interpersonal (group work)
11:00–12:30	Lunch and Specials	N/A	N/A
12:30–1:45	Reading/Language Arts	Had students complete silent reading of book *There's an Owl in the Shower* by Jean Craighead George. Asked students to write their opinion of saving endangered animals like the spotted owls.	1. Verbal-Linguistic 2. Naturalistic 3. Existential
1:45–2:00	Wrap Down Time	Went over assignments for week and month. Emphasis on how to plan time for final project to be completed on time.	1. Logical-Mathematical 2. Verbal-Linguistic
2:00	Dismissal	N/A	N/A

Using My Multiple Intelligences During the Day

Self-Observation

Date of observation: ______________________________

Time	Class Taught	Description of Activity and/or Materials Used	Multiple Intelligence(s) Used by Teacher

Setting Some Goals

Once you engage in self-observation, you'll begin to recognize which of the intelligences you bring into the classroom and which ones you underutilize. The next step is to identify ways to use those weaker intelligences more fully as you teach. Below are goals set by nine different teachers. Each has recognized an intelligence he or she tends to neglect in the classroom. Then each has formulated a specific, manageable goal to incorporate that intelligence into his or her teaching repertoire.

Sample Goals for Incorporating Multiple Intelligences Into Teaching Practice

Verbal-Linguistic intelligence—Beth, a second-grade teacher

Observation:

I have always been a shy person and I do not really enjoy reading. When I observed myself for several days, I saw that I actually create numerous learning centers where I do not have to speak much.

Goal #1:

My goal is more direct teaching. I will begin with science lessons, and prepare lectures that also incorporate some of Howard Gardner's multiple intelligences. Even though I will use visuals and music, I will primarily present out loud to the students starting with 10 minutes a day during science time.

Goal #2:

Even though I was never a good reader, I do want my students to be good readers. In order for me to develop a love of books that I can convey to my students, I plan to start reading mysteries, one after the other.

Logical-Mathematical intelligence—Sheila, a kindergarten teacher

Observation:

I knew before taking the Alert questionnaire that I would be a strong right-brain person. I know that I have always been able to feel and sense the correct answers. I was not surprised to find the logical-mathematical intelligence an underdeveloped area. It all makes sense.

Goal:

So what to do, what to do? How do I become more left-brained? More logically inclined? I know, I will start to work off lists and outlines. I will use outlines at home, and I will put outlines on the board for my students. This will help them see the logical order of the day.

Spatial intelligence—Marc, a fourth-grade teacher

Observation:

I turned out to be left brain on the Alert test, so it was not a surprise for me to see that I seem to avoid using visuals when I teach. I can see now that many students would learn more efficiently if I used visuals when I lecture.

Goal #1:

My first goal is to use overheads each time I present a lesson to the class. This will help me use spatial intelligence when I teach.

Goal #2:

My second goal is something I have been wanting to do for over a year: to learn PowerPoint so that I can give PowerPoint presentations to the students. And later, I'd like to teach my students how to make PowerPoint presentations themselves.

Musical intelligence—Sally, a sixth-grade history teacher

Observation:

It is interesting that although I really love music, I have never considered using it at school. I play the piano and sing in the church choir. I often listen to the radio and CDs when I am at home. How odd not to use this strength of mine when I teach.

Goal:

My goal is to bring music into my classroom. Just thinking about it, I can see that it will brighten the day for all of us. I will start using music with our ancient history lessons. I think the students would benefit from hearing how music was played before pianos were invented. From now on, I will associate the music with each period of time in history that I teach.

Bodily-Kinesthetic intelligence—Kayla, a first-grade teacher

Observation:

After observing myself, I saw that I tend not to use the bodily-kinesthetic intelligence during the day. This is an intelligence that is underdeveloped for me. I never voluntarily joined in group sports, I did not go out for cheerleading. To this day I do not enjoy dancing. How to incorporate this into my day at school when I really do not like it myself?

Goal:

Kayla wrote that she asked another first-grade teacher for suggestions and came up with this goal: My goal to incorporate the bodily-kinesthetic intelligence into the first grade will be through my arithmetic lessons. I will let the students get up and move. When I teach that four plus four equals eight, I will let two groups of four get together, and let the class count all of them. *Then* I will write the equation on the board.

Interpersonal intelligence—Joyce, a fourth-grade teacher

Observation:

Being the left-brain lady that I am, I tend to lecture, present, and encourage discussion for most of the day. For the students, this method primarily uses their intrapersonal intelligence. I always preferred to work on my own in high school and college. I assumed that my students were like me.

Goal:

My goal is to assign class projects with group work at least three times a week, as this will benefit students who actually prefer to work in groups. I think that language arts is the best class in which to begin this experiment.

Intrapersonal intelligence

—Paul, a middle school teacher

Observation:

For most of the school day, my students are divided into groups. This uses the interpersonal intelligence. I find it interesting that I, too, like to learn in groups. In college, I was always happiest when my professor assigned group projects.

Goal:

My goal is to assign independent work during the day in order to meet the needs of my students who learn in an intrapersonal manner. I plan to start this by creating a minimum of two independent assignments a week. If this goes well, I will consider assigning more individual work.

Naturalistic intelligence

—Mark, a third-grade teacher

Observation:

Upon reflection, I see that I am basically an "indoors" type of person. I play basketball indoors, I work out indoors, I like to read and explore on my computer. I do not take my class outside for any lessons.

Goal:

In a month, we are slated to have a lesson on rocks and minerals. I will borrow some rock hammers and take the class to the park where we will collect sedimentary and metamorphic rock samples. I bet that I will be able to think of other ways to get them outside.

Existential intelligence

—Pam, a second-grade teacher

Observation:

I tend to be very busy during the day, rushing here and there. I am goal-oriented and take pride in accomplishing many goals. I do not take time to consider the existential end of things in my life at home or at school.

Goal:

I now see that most of my students will benefit from reflecting on pertinent existential issues. I plan to incorporate existential questions and reflections into my reading lessons on a daily basis.

Now it's your turn to set some of your own multiple intelligence goals. Setting goals begins with self-observation. What intelligences do you underutilize when teaching? How might you stretch to exercise those intelligences in the classroom? Use the form on page 87 to set your own goals.

In the next section we'll look at how to apply the multiple intelligences with your students.

Exploring Your Students' Multiple Intelligences

Gardner's work has inspired thousands of teachers to expand their lesson plans, create thematic units, and make active attempts to include all of their students by incorporating multiple perspectives.

Perhaps the greatest contribution of Gardner's theory is best expressed by Scherer (1997) who states, "When intelligence is defined in the plural, adults and other children treat children who are smart in unconventional ways more respectfully" (p. 7).

Many teachers like to give their students multiple intelligence questionnaires like the Connell Multiple Intelligence Questionnaire for Children on page 87. It's fascinating to see how the class breaks down in terms of their strong, moderate, and underdeveloped various intelligences.

The results can help you shape lesson plans during the year. For example, if you see that there are more than the usual numbers of students with naturalistic strengths, you can plan more outdoor activities. If you have a lot of students with existential and intrapersonal intelligences, you may want to create more inspirational and self-reflecting lessons. Consult the lists on pages 77–79 for ideas for each intelligence.

It is exciting for students to see the areas that they are strongest in, and to understand how these might be affecting their schoolwork. For example, let's say Sarah is the best reader in your third-grade class, but one of the slowest in arithmetic. It would stand to reason that she would be highly developed in the verbal-linguistic area but underdeveloped in the logical-mathematical area. If she takes the multiple intelligences test and sees this is the case, and you explain that people can develop their weaker intelligences with extra attention and practice, perhaps she will agree to stay after school and work two afternoons a week on her arithmetic so that she can catch up.

Goal Setting

Multiple Intelligence Goal #1

Self-Observation

Goal

Multiple Intelligence Goal #2

Self-Observation

Goal

Multiple Intelligence Goal #3

Self-Observation

Goal

The Connell Multiple Intelligence Questionnaire for Children

Put a check next to each sentence that describes you.

Area 1

_____ I like to listen to songs on the radio or a CD.
_____ I like to watch music videos on TV.
_____ I like to go to music concerts and hear live music.
_____ I can easily remember tunes, raps, or melodies.
_____ I take music lessons, singing lessons, or play a musical instrument.
_____ I can learn new songs easily.
_____ I like to sing.

Area 2

_____ I like art classes.
_____ I like to draw, paint, and make things with clay.
_____ I enjoy putting puzzles together.
_____ I like to build things using blocks, Legos, and models.
_____ It is fun to play video games.
_____ I can create a picture in my mind to help me think things through.
_____ I notice the different styles of things, such as clothes, cars, and hairstyles.

Area 3

_____ I like to read books, magazines, and comic books.
_____ I have a good vocabulary and like to learn new words.
_____ I enjoy writing e-mails to my friends.
_____ I like to write.
_____ It is fun to play word games such as Scrabble and Mad Libs, do crossword puzzles, and acrostics.
_____ I think it would be fun to keep a journal of my thoughts and ideas.
_____ I like to talk to my friends on the telephone.

Area 4

_____ I like to play with animals and take care of them.
_____ I like going to zoos, parks, or aquariums.
_____ I like being outside.
_____ I like to hike, walk, or run outdoors.
_____ I like to observe nature's changes, such as thunderstorms, rain, snow, and sunshine.
_____ I help to recycle and take care of our environment.
_____ I pay close attention to things in my environment such as trees, rocks, flowers, birds, bugs, and squirrels.

Area 5

_____ I like to do science experiments and go to science museums.
_____ I find arithmetic and math problems interesting.
_____ It is fun to solve mysteries.
_____ Numbers are really interesting to me.
_____ I like games like chess or computer games where you have to think a lot.
_____ I like TV shows like *ZOOM*, *National Geographic*, and *Nova* that talk about science and math.
_____ I can do math problems in my head and make good estimates.

Area 6

_____ I like to dance.
_____ I like to play sports such as baseball, soccer, hockey, or football.
_____ I like to build models or do beading, sewing, macramé, or carpentry.
_____ I enjoy acting in plays or skits or playing charades.
_____ I like to move when I am thinking about things.
_____ I like activities such as the martial arts, tennis, running, jogging, biking, skateboarding, or gymnastics.
_____ I can sometimes "feel" the right answer.

Area 7

_____ I like to be with my friends often.
_____ I like to help those who need help.
_____ I like to read books or see movies about people and their lives.
_____ I can usually tell how other people are feeling.
_____ It is fun for me to organize activities at home and at school.
_____ I would rather spend time with others than spend time alone.
_____ I like to talk in class discussions.

Area 8

_____ I like doing things by myself.
_____ I would rather work by myself than with other students.
_____ I like to spend time thinking or writing about things that matter to me.
_____ I like to play computer games.
_____ I usually know what my feelings are.
_____ I like to write my thoughts and feelings in a diary or journal.
_____ I know what things I am good at, and what things I am not so good at.

Scoring—Count up the number of responses you had for each area. The areas that you check show how you are smart in the different areas.

_____ = Area 1 (Music Smart)
_____ = Area 2 (Picture Smart)
_____ = Area 3 (Word Smart)
_____ = Area 4 (Nature Smart)
_____ = Area 5 (Math Smart)
_____ = Area 6 (Body Smart)
_____ = Area 7 (People Smart)
_____ = Area 8 (Self Smart)

A score of 5 or more indicates a very strong area; a score of 3–4 indicates a moderate area; and a score of less than 3 indicates a developing area.

I have found Armstrong's books (see bibliography) extremely helpful when setting up a multiple intelligence classroom or designing multiple intelligence lessons. For students in grades kindergarten to fourth, Armstrong's "translations" of Gardner's multiple intelligences are easier to understand than Gardner's original designations. They are listed in Table 5.1.

Table 5.1 Multiple Intelligences and Translations

Howard Gardner's Multiple Intelligences	**Thomas Armstrong's Applications**
1. Verbal-Linguistic	1. Word Smart
2. Logical-Mathematical	2. Math Smart
3. Spatial	3. Picture Smart
4. Bodily-Kinesthetic	4. Body Smart
5. Musical	5. Music Smart
6. Interpersonal	6. People Smart
7. Intrapersonal	7. Self Smart
8. Naturalistic	8. Nature Smart
9. Existential	9. Spiritual Smart*

** I added this entry to balance the table.*

Armstrong suggests teaching students about multiple intelligences using the multiple intelligence pie. In this scenario, a pie is cut into nine slices, one for each intelligence. A fun variation would be to have the students make their own circle, where each of the nine wedges is in proportion to the strength of the particular intelligences that person possesses; See Table 5.2. For example, if Robert were strongest in the bodily-kinesthetic, logical-mathematical, and spatial intelligences, then these wedges would be the largest on his circle. Other helpful books include *Developing Students Multiple Intelligences* by Kristen Nicholson Nelson (1998) and *Teaching and Learning Through Multiple Intelligence* by Linda Campbell, Bruce Campbell, and Dee Dickinson (1996).

Table 5.2 Kids' Multiple Intelligence Circle

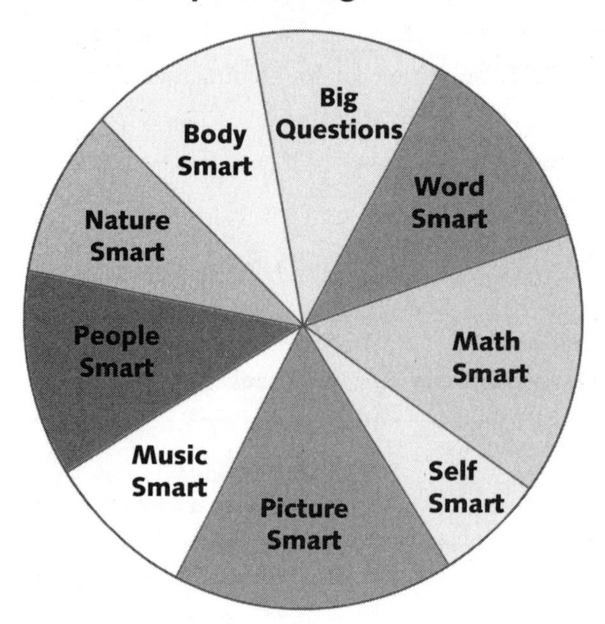

Adapted from Thomas Armstrong's Multiple Intelligence Pie

Thematic Teaching and Multiple Intelligences

Ideally, we would incorporate all of the multiple intelligences into our lessons and offer students choices in assignments, in order to reach and engage all of our students. But how do we do this? Thematic teaching is one effective and manageable way.

Thematic teaching allows you to teach required content to all students while allowing individuals to further investigate areas of particular interest to them. It's easy to incorporate a variety of assignments that are linked to the theme but enable students to explore the content in ways that appeal to them, which are often linked to their multiple intelligences. In this way, we achieve what Gardner refers to as "more depth, less breadth." Thematic teaching expands the way our students learn and aids in helping our students connect to prior knowledge. When we link music with language arts, our lessons suddenly come alive in the classroom—and in the brain, two separate neural passageways will connect to form a superhighway.

To see how to make a thematic unit work, let's think through a thematic unit on life cycles. The overarching goal is for students to understand that living things grow and change over the course of their lives. The specific science content students must learn is the life cycle of the butterfly. Given these objectives, let's consider the assignments and activities we could offer that would assure that students would learn the content in a meaningful way.

Thematic Unit Planning Sheet

Topic: *Life Cycles*

Goal: *Students will understand that living things grow and change over the course of their lives. Students will learn about the life cycle of a butterfly.*

Potential Assignments/Activities by Intelligence

Verbal-Linguistic Intelligence

- *Lecture on topic of life cycles in general and butterfly life cycle in particular (whole class).*
- *Guide discussions about life cycles (whole class or small group).*
- *Assign students to research and present information on the life cycle of another animal or plant (individual, pairs, small group).*

Logical-Mathematical Intelligence

- *Have students analyze the six major categories of butterflies as well as examine the butterflies of the world (individual or small group).*
- *Have students compare and contrast the life cycle of a butterfly to that of another insect or animal (individual, small group).*
- *Have students represent the life cycle of a butterfly (or other living thing) on a timeline (individual, small group).*

Spatial Intelligence

- *Show a movie on the life cycle of a butterfly (whole class).*
- *Have students create posters depicting the life cycle of a butterfly (individual, small group).*

Musical Intelligence

- *Have students write a song about the life cycle of a butterfly, or other animal or plant (individual or small group).*
- *Play flute music and invite students to imagine butterflies flying on a warm spring day (whole class).*

- *Invite musical students to play a piece on their instrument that resembles soft, happy butterfly music (individual).*

Bodily-Kinesthetic Intelligence

- *Have students act out the life cycle of a butterfly or other animal. (small group).*
- *Invite students to dance the way a butterfly flies (whole class, small group).*

Interpersonal Intelligence

- *Provide opportunities for group work. Several ideas listed can be done in groups.*

Intrapersonal Intelligence

- *Provide a reflective assignment, preferably toward the end of the unit, after the class has observed the metamorphosis. Ask students to write about what they would like to change into if they could. To combine two intelligences here, students could first write about what they'd like to change into and then play music in the background as they read their presentation to the class. For instance, if they want to morph into a lion they could put on drums! (individual).*

Naturalistic Intelligence

- *Use a butterfly kit. Kits come with either eggs or caterpillars, and the metamorphosis time will vary. Selecting a kit that starts with eggs will enable students to observe all four stages of development in the life cycle of a butterfly egg, larva, pupa, and adult butterfly. Students will get to witness firsthand the developmental stages in the life cycle of a butterfly (whole class).*
- *Visit butterfly exhibit at local zoo (whole class).*

Existential Intelligence

- *Assign a reflective essay in which students consider: What type of person are you now? What type of adult would you like to become? (individual).*

After brainstorming activities and assignments, compare your ideas with your curriculum, available materials, and the preferences of your students. The final lesson plan might look something like this.

Thematic Lesson Outline

Topic: Life Cycles

Timeframe: Three periods/week for three weeks (to watch larvae grow to butterflies)

Day 1: Introduce topic of life cycles. Brief lecture and show film on life cycle of butterflies. Open and explain butterfly kit. Have students write observations of larvae in journal. (verbal-linguistic, spatial, naturalistic)

Day 2: Discuss life cycles of other insects, animals, and plants. Have students work in a small group to choose an animal or plant to research. Groups decide which topic to research and how they will present their information. (verbal-linguistic, interpersonal)

Day 3: Students conduct research in library. (verbal-linguistic, logical-mathematical, interpersonal)

Day 4: Students write observations of butterfly kit. Students prepare presentation of research (see options on page 94). (verbal-linguistic, logical-mathematical, interpersonal)

Day 5: Groups present research. (varies by project)

Day 6: Groups present research. (varies by project)

Day 7: Students write observations of butterfly kit. Brief lecture on metamorphosis. Play flute music and invite students to flit like butterflies. Assign butterfly project; students can work individually or in pairs. (verbal-linguistic, logical-mathematical, musical, bodily-kinesthetic)

Day 8: Students work on butterfly project. (varies by project)

Day 9: Students present butterfly projects and complete in-class essay. (verbal-linguistic)

A lot of teachers tell me they have the most trouble thinking up activities to cover the existential area. I have found repeatedly that it is well worth the effort. The students in your classroom who are either intrapersonal and/or existential will be extremely grateful that at least a portion of the unit is reflective.

Research Project: Life Cycles

Choose a plant or animal. Research its life cycle, using books, magazines, encyclopedias, and the Internet as sources.

What questions do you have about your plant or animal's life cycle? Record your questions and answers in your science journal; be sure to include the source of information.

Next, decide how you will share the information you have learned with your classmates. Choose one option from each of the following groups of activities:

Summarize the Information

- *Write an essay describing the life cycle.*
- *Prepare a poster that illustrates the life cycle.*

Present the Information in a Memorable Way

- *Write and perform a poem or song describing the life cycle.*
- *Act out the life cycle.*

Butterfly Project

Choose one of the following options to demonstrate your learning about the life cycle of butterflies. You may work on your own or with a partner.

1. *Prepare a poster that illustrates the life cycle of a butterfly.*
2. *Represent the life cycle of a butterfly on a timeline.*
3. *Write and illustrate a nonfiction book about the life cycle of butterflies for kindergartners.*

In-Class Essay Choices

What have you learned about life cycles from this unit? Use specific examples from our study of butterflies and your research project.

Compare and contrast the life cycle of a butterfly to that of another animal you've learned about in this unit (from your own research or from a classmate's presentation).

Think about the concept of metamorphosis. What kind of big change would you like to see happen in your life as you grow older? Describe how this fits in with your own life cycle.

A Multiple Intelligence Lesson Plan in Action

During the spring of 1999, I designed and implemented a series of 10 brain-based learning lessons for third-grade students. These took place on Fridays and became known as "Literary Fridays." There were 22 third graders in an inclusion classroom at the Abbot School in Westford, Massachusetts. The students with special needs had learning disabilities, speech and language deficits, and emotional disorders. Each brain-based lesson was one and a half hours long.

My goal was to incorporate brain-based learning techniques into my lessons in order to reach all students, with their particular multiple intelligence strengths, in an inclusion classroom.

The 10 Literary Friday lessons were based on multiple intelligence theory—I used as many of Gardner's nine intelligences as possible in each of these lessons.

For seven of the 10 lessons, I used books written and illustrated by Patricia Polacco. These books were chosen because they contain excellent illustrations, rich historical and naturalistic references, as well as strong emotional components. Polacco's books examine brother-sister relationships, grandparent-grandchild relationships, multiracial relationships, and religion. Her books lay a rich foundation from which we can build a strong multiple intelligence lesson. The following lesson was one of the 10 Literary Friday lessons presented to Mrs. Fisher's third-grade class. The theme of this lesson was special relationships.

At the Rivier College Early Childhood Center, teachers are required to write weekly multiple intelligence units. Each intelligence is assigned its own color. Teachers use color markers to highlight each activity to be sure that each intelligence is used regularly. The colors also signal if a teacher is either overusing, or under-using one of the intelligences.

Theme: Special Relationships

Materials Needed:

1. Book—*Mrs. Katz and Tush* by Patricia Polacco. This book gently explores a growing relationship between an elderly Jewish woman, Mrs. Katz, and an African-American family, especially focusing upon Larnel who is around eight years old when the story opens. Tush is the kitten that

Larnel gives to Mrs. Katz because she seems lonely. A meaningful relationship develops as Larnel and Mrs. Katz get to know one another better and appreciate their different cultures.

2. A clipboard with:
   a. new vocabulary words: words that the students will hear in the story but are not likely to know.
   b. questions and ideas for discussion.
   c. the phrase "You're such a person" (which is an important phrase in the book) written out on a card, with added decoration.
3. CD player and CD of *The King and I*
4. Words to the song "Getting to Know You" photocopied for each student
5. Book with pictures of a Manx cat
6. Food and drinks pertaining to the story (kugel, matzo, spicy apples, or other Passover food)
7. Templates for "Such a Person" dolls with buttons for eyes, yarn for hair, and wallpaper for clothes

Lesson Overview

The following describes the components of the 90-minute lesson. Each section was designed to appeal to students strong in different intelligences.

Introducing the Lesson

I sat in a chair with the students sitting on the floor by me. I showed them the cover and said, "This book has a theme about a very special and unusual relationship. Understanding and appreciating different types of relationships can change your life." Then I asked them, "What types of important relationships do you have in your life right now? What makes them so special?"

The conversation began with one girl telling the group that her parents were her "best and most special relationship." Another child said, "My dad died so my mom is my most important relationship, but Granny and Pappy are also special to me, too."

Next, I introduced two to four new vocabulary words that were important to the story but that might be unfamiliar to students. I typed them in large, bold print and glued them to a decorated chart. We discussed the meaning of the words, and then I read the story, pausing to show the illustrations on each page.

Discussing Theme

I prepared questions about three themes from the story:

(a) *Loneliness*

Mrs. Katz had lost her husband and had no children. Questions included: *Why do you suppose Larnel gave her the kitten? Larnel seemed lonely too; why do you suppose they became such good friends? Have you ever felt lonely? When was that?*

(b) *Prejudice*

We discussed why some people feel prejudice. Questions included: *How would you feel if someone was prejudiced against you? What would you do if you saw someone act prejudiced toward a friend?*

(c) *Friendship*

We discussed the importance of friendships. Questions included: *Do any of you have friends at a completely different age level, or from a different ethnicity, like Mrs. Katz and Larnel? How can friendships change our lives?*

I used these questions to launch and guide a meaningful discussion of the story, helping students make personal connections to it.

After our discussion, I showed students a poster I had made of the phrase, "You're such a person," taken from the book. We discussed it within the context of the story and our own lives.

Integrating the Content-Area Learning

Using a reference book, I showed students some pictures of Manx cats and discussed why these cats do not have tails.

Then I used a globe to locate Poland for the students. (Mrs. Katz is from Poland.) We discussed the fact that so many people have come to America from other countries. I asked the students if they knew from which country their grandparents or great-grandparents came.

Additionally, because Mrs. Katz has Larnel over for a Passover seder, we discussed aspects of Passover.

Deepening Understanding Through Multiple Intelligences

After discussing the phrase "You're such a person," I told the class, "Each and every one of you is becoming 'such a person' to Mrs. Fisher and me! We want to sing a song to you to illustrate this point. I will pass out the words to the song, and Mrs. Fisher and I will sing it to you the first time. Then you can join in and sing it the second time." I turned on the CD and together Mrs. Fisher and I danced and sang the words to "Getting to Know You" from *The King and I*.

The students loved it! We played the song a third time, and we all moved to the music!

Tying It All Together

For a culminating activity, I had each child cut out and decorate a template of someone they felt was "such a person." They decorated the person with crayons, yarn, eye buttons, and so on. On the back of the template, students wrote why the person was so special to them.

At the end of the lesson, we offered refreshments. The students got gingerbread men and juice, and continued our discussion of "such a person" and special people in our lives.

On the day of the last Literary Friday, Mrs. Fisher and her class presented me with a golden gift bag filled with 23 beautifully decorated thank-you letters and flowers. Around my birthday, I also received 23 handmade birthday cards—each with a special drawing, message, and/or gift. One boy, with identified emotional disorders, had drawn a picture of me holding the large CD player I brought in each day, which seemed to confirm my observations that he had strong musical intelligence. A girl with learning disabilities wrote: "We enjoyed everything you gave us to do and to listen about. I love your enthuseum and your pashens. I will never never forget you working in our classroom." This experience confirmed for me the value of incorporating multiple intelligences into my lesson plans.

Looking Ahead

My hope is that both you and your students will benefit from understanding your moderate and highly developed intelligences, and enjoy working to enhance your underdeveloped ones. Remember Bruce Campbell's observation that his own undeveloped intelligences increased when he used them with his students.

In Chapter Six, we will focus on the theory of information processing—how we learn. Then in Chapter Seven, we will focus on learning styles, which are based on Information Processing theory. You can take three questionnaires to see your receptive, processing, and expressive learning style, as well as examine ways to teach our students to keep their learning style preferences in mind.

Chapter 6

Information Processing Theory

"The knowledge in our minds consists of neuronal networks in our brains, so if that knowledge is to grow, the neuronal networks must physically change."

—James Zull (2002, p. 112)

How does our brain learn new information? Do we have a preferred way of learning? These questions will be answered in this chapter and in Chapter Seven. Here, we will examine the components of information processing, which enable us to understand how we learn and remember. Our preferences for how we receive, process, and express information can be thought of as our learning style. Chapter Seven focuses on teacher and student learning styles. It contains learning style questionnaires and suggestions for brain-based learning lessons and activities.

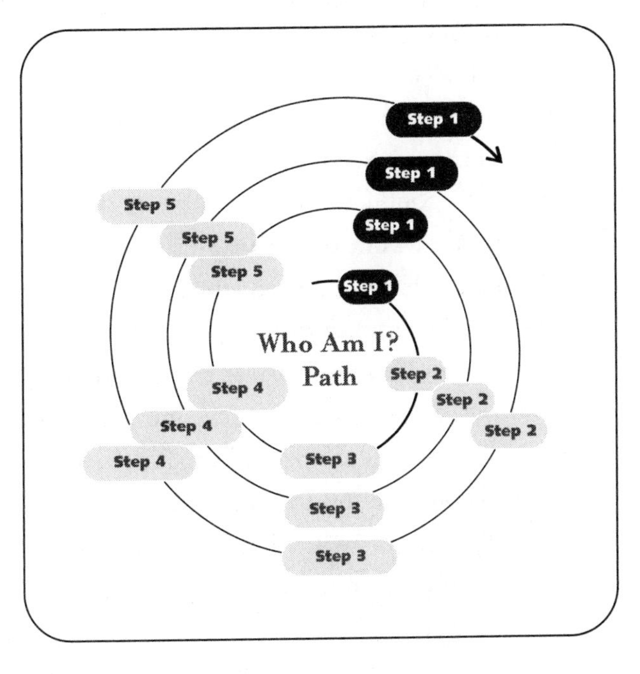

Figure 6.1 Information Processing Model

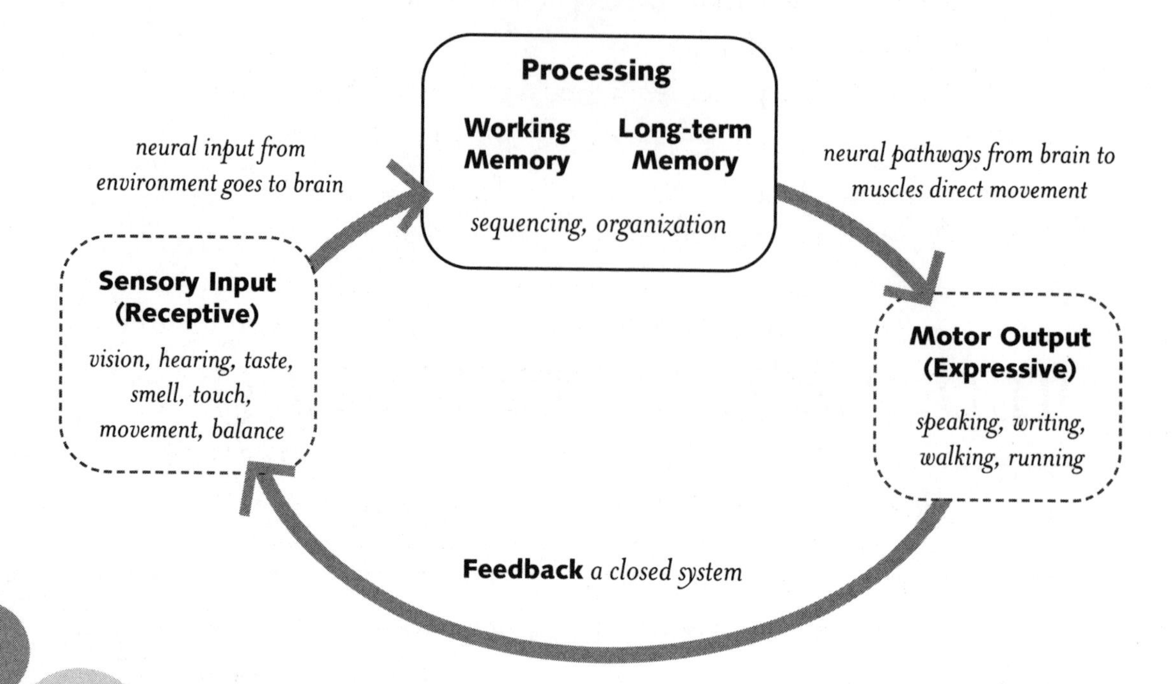

Information Processing

Information processing theory traces the flow of information during the learning process (see Figure 6.1). It is modeled on what engineers describe as an "input-output" model. For example, with a computer, input devices would be the keyboard or the mouse; the processing would be the modem or the central processing unit of the computer; output devices would be the computer screen or the printer. Bruce Goldstein (2005) reports that research conducted in the 1950s and 1960s, which compared the ways computers work to the way human beings process information, brought forth the development of the information processing approach and a focus on cognitive psychology.

How students learn is of interest to teachers at all grade levels. The theory of information processing provides a focus on how students learn, process, and remember information. Preston Feden and Robert Vogel (2003) provide the following big ideas of information processing theory (p. 45). These ideas will be explored throughout Chapters Six and Seven.

1. Stimuli from the environment impinge upon our senses.
2. What we recognize and pay attention to moves on to our working memory.
3. What we neither recognize nor pay attention to decays.

4. Once in working memory, we rehearse information to maintain it long enough to decide whether or not we want to process it further or more deeply.
5. That which we process further is encoded into long-term memory.
6. That which we do not process further is often forgotten.
7. Information in long-term memory is then available to be retrieved, when necessary, in order for us to make a cognitive response.

Information processing can be divided into three main stages: receptive, which describes how sensory information (input) comes from the environment into our brain; processing, which describes how our brain organizes and remembers the sensory information; and expressive, which describes how our brain sends messages to our muscles, which then cause us to move (see the graph below). In essence, we receive information from our environment, process it, and then act on it, changing the environment and creating new sensory inputs. It's a continuous cycle. In education, we can think of these three stages as a learning loop. Students receive information (from a lecture, or reading, for example). Then they organize it in their minds, connecting it to what they already know. Ultimately, they act on the new information, by answering a question on a test, perhaps, or by preparing a presentation. We'll examine each of these information processing stages in more depth.

Receiving Sensory Input

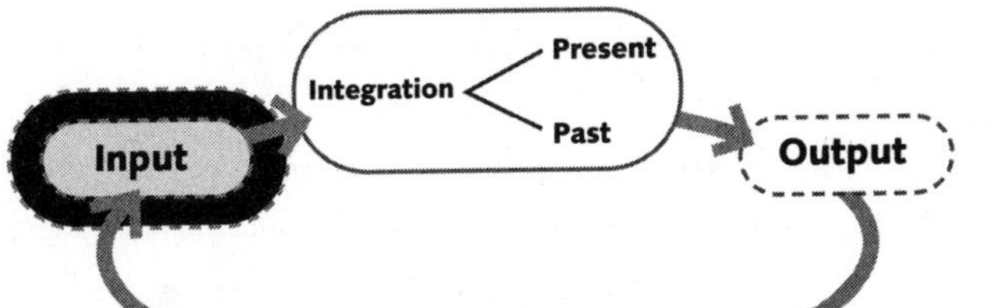

In the receptive stage, the brain receives input from outside of our body via our senses. Researcher Newell Kephart (1971) defines sensory input as "a translation of outside energy into patterns of neural impulses" (p. 108). These neural impulses travel from our sensory organs up to specific areas in the brain lobes.

Information Processing

How We Learn New Information

Human beings are constantly bombarded by environmental stimuli (Feden and Vogel, 2003). Depending on our location, at any given moment our brain receives between approximately 50 and 2,000 sensory messages. There will be significantly more sensory input for our brain to sort out if we are walking through a busy intersection in New York City than if we are at home in our bedroom reading. Stop for a moment. Think about the sensory inputs you are receiving at this very moment: What can you see other than the words of this book? What sounds can you hear? Are you drinking coffee? Eating popcorn? Smelling brownies cooking in the oven? Chewing gum? Listening to music? Watching television? Shaking your lower leg? Feeling a shoe that is laced too tightly? If you really think about it, you will be amazed at the amount of sensory data that our brain must sort through at any given moment. We tend to ignore most of this information in order to focus on the task at hand.

These days, people refer to our seven senses, not just five. Researchers have discovered that we possess a sense of movement, called the proprioceptive system, and a sense of balance, called the vestibular system (Smith and Gouze, 2004). These systems are referred to as the "hidden senses" because they tend to operate at an unconscious level. Karen Smith and Karen Gouze (2004) define the proprioceptive sense as our "body position sense." This sense helps us integrate movement and touch sensations in our bodies. When your students sit down at their desks, they depend upon their sense of proprioception to provide feedback to their body in order to remain seated and not fall off the chair. Carol Stock Kranowitz (2003) defines the vestibular sense as the system that lets us maintain balance by coordinating movements in our eyes, head, and body. The vestibular sense is critical in forming the relationship of a person to gravity and the physical world. It responds to changes in the positioning of our head and to our body as we move. Our vestibular sense is critical in forming the relationship of a person to gravity and the physical world.

Table 6.1 summarizes the seven sensory systems. We continually receive sensory input from each of these systems.

Everyday Sensory Inputs

I used to teach at Northeastern University in Boston, Massachusetts. Walking out of the classroom building to get to my office off of Huntington Avenue often constituted an overload of sensory input. On the visual end alone, I could see numerous vehicles moving along the two-sided road, trolleys clanked up and down Huntington Avenue, making several stops at Northeastern University. On warm, sunny days, there were food vendors on the sidewalks, people walking, talking, and laughing; there were often students on skateboards and bicycles. I could see hundreds of people walking, reading, and studying. Occasionally I saw a class meeting outdoors. All of these are just the visual inputs.

Table 6.1 Sensory Systems

Sense	Definition	Description
1. Auditory	Sense of Hearing	There are many tiny hairs in our inner ear that "respond to specific vibrations by stimulating specific nerve endings" (Hannaford, 1995, p. 38). This allows us to discriminate between different sounds.
2. Visual	Sense of Seeing	"Our eyes are designed to move and accommodate for light, to give us as much sensory detail about our world as possible" (Hannaford, 1995, p. 46). Visual information goes from our eyes to the occipital lobes in our left and right hemispheres.
3. Olfactory	Sense of Smell	There are many tiny hairs inside the nose that stimulate olfactory nerves for individual smells.
4. Gustatory	Sense of Taste	Our taste buds are grouped on the tongue. Each taste bud contains a number of receptor cells that send messages to the thalamus, and then onto the cortex, where we become aware of the actual taste.
5. Tactile	Sense of Touch	Tactile information is received from sensory cells called receptors. They are located on our skin all over our body.
6. Proprioceptive System	Sense of Movement	Proprioceptors send information up to our brain from our bones, joints, and muscles.
7. Vestibular System	Sense of Balance	Located in the inner ear, the vestibular system is stimulated by our head, eye, neck, and body movements. The vestibular system coordinates movements of our eyes, head, neck, and body.

As for auditory inputs, I could hear trolleys and buses screeching, cars honking, and the taxicab drivers yelling. The food vendors would call out to advertise their offerings, and the college students would giggle excitedly.

Olfactory sensations (often unpleasant) bombarded my system through my nose. On my walks, I could almost always smell vehicle exhaust and the oily trolley. In the spring and autumn, it was a relief to focus on the aromas of warm hot dogs and pretzels and perfumed flowers in bloom.

Kinesthetically, I would always have to be aware of where I was walking so as not to bump into people, vendors, skateboards, bicycles, and so on. I had to rely on two systems:

- *Vestibular:* It was often challenging to walk with dignity and balance, as I constantly had to dodge pedestrians, joggers, and skateboards.
- *Proprioceptive:* When I was walking close to the street, I had to be sure not to accidentally slip off of the sidewalk and into the incoming street traffic.

And all of this is typical of anyone living in a relatively densely populated area. You can see that during many moments on a typical day, the average person encounters thousands of sensory stimuli.

Sensory Inputs in the Classroom

Now admittedly, there were a lot of sensory inputs that my poor brain had to deal with on Huntington Avenue as I walked to my office, but let's compare this to the constant barrage of sensory inputs found in a typical classroom.

First, let's consider visual input. Let's assume there are roughly 24 people in the classroom. Each has different hair color, skin color, and clothing. They are different heights and weight. Some have glasses, some don't. Some wear watches, some don't. Desks and chairs, tables, chalkboards, whiteboards, computers, reading books, reference books, and posters abound. Student projects are mounted on the walls and hanging from the ceiling. Visually there are thousands of inputs coming into the brain of each of your students at any given moment.

Next, let's consider auditory input. What noises do your students typically hear? Chairs scraping against the floor, chalk scratching against the chalkboard, or markers squeaking against a whiteboard are typical sounds heard in the classroom. The teacher may be talking, students may be whispering. Students are often flipping through pages in a book or rummaging through their desks, searching for something. Sometimes the principal makes an announcement over the loudspeaker; in some classrooms the telephone may ring. Perhaps noises come in from outside—traffic if you are in the city, bird calls if you are in a country school.

Even without going over the remaining five senses, we can easily see that at any given moment, even in the classroom setting, the brain has to deal with hundreds to thousands of sensory inputs. What does the brain do with all of this incoming information? How do we process it? How do we remember? This is the domain of the brain's processing function, which we will explore next.

Processing Sensory Input

The second stage in the learning loop is processing sensory information. This stage involves processing, integrating, organizing, learning, and remembering information received through our senses. Many neural connections are formed and enhanced as we process new information.

How does our brain process all of the sensory information that is continually pouring into it? First and foremost, our brain must constantly sort out the relevant from the irrelevant sensory information. For example, I did not try and memorize the color and the license plates of all the cars that I saw every day passing by on Huntington Avenue. Students need not memorize what their teacher or their classmates are wearing on any given day. So, what can you do to help your students focus on what is relevant?

In order to learn, the brain must attend to relevant stimuli. Many students, especially those with learning disabilities and attention deficit disorder, have trouble differentiating between relevant and irrelevant stimuli. For example, Jason hears Luna cough and gets distracted from listening to the teacher explain double-digit addition. Jason may start to think about when he was sick last week and subsequently miss the entire presentation. Most students will tune out Luna's cough, knowing that it is more important to focus on and listen to the teacher. Sometimes, though, it is good to help cue our students when to listen. Here are some suggestions for cueing students to pay attention and helping them to focus on relevant stimuli:

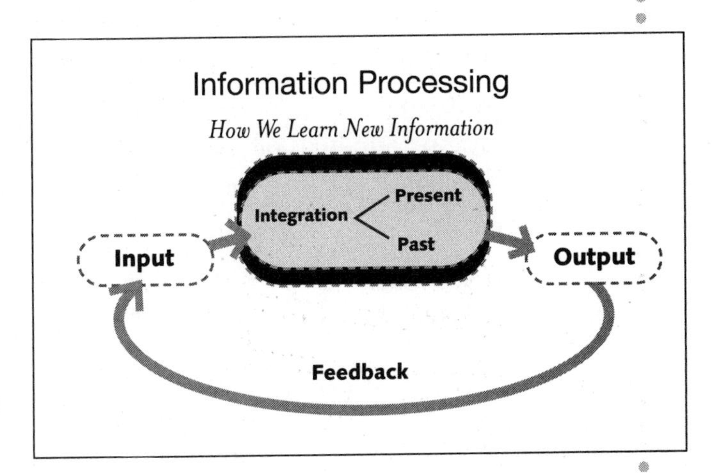

- Say, "I'd like all eyes and ears on me," and then proceed to make a point.
- Underscore a key idea by saying, "What I just said is an important point; please write it in your notebooks."
- Write key points on the chalkboard as you talk. These should be words for the left-brain learners and with visual maps for the right brain learners. (Do both simultaneously.)
- Write the important points that students make on the board or the overhead. Writing provides a big clue that what was said is worthy of students' attention.
- Make all content relevant to your students' lives. For example, when I am teaching the undergraduate assessment course, I tell students that, as teachers, they will be required to attend, and participate in special education team meetings. I explain to them that they need to understand the test data in order to understand how their students learn. The point being that when we deliberately show students the connection between the material they are learning and their life outside the classroom, they will pay attention.

Once the brain selects the relevant stimuli, there are three critically important functions that it must perform. First, the brain must organize the information. Second, it must sequence the information, and third, it must make the information available for recall (Kephart, 1971). Being a left-brain learner, I like to think of information as being organized, sequenced, and remembered linearly in thousands of file folders all neatly organized and sorted in drawers that I can pull out as needed. In actuality, though, information flows. A more accurate image would be something like this: imagine hundreds of thousands of roads, neural connections, all intersecting at different places. There are a multitude of roads, byways, highways, intersections, bridges, and even superhighways. But just how do we actually organize and store information so we can remember and use it? We must move it into long-term memory, discussed in the next section.

Attention, Working Memory, and Long-Term Memory

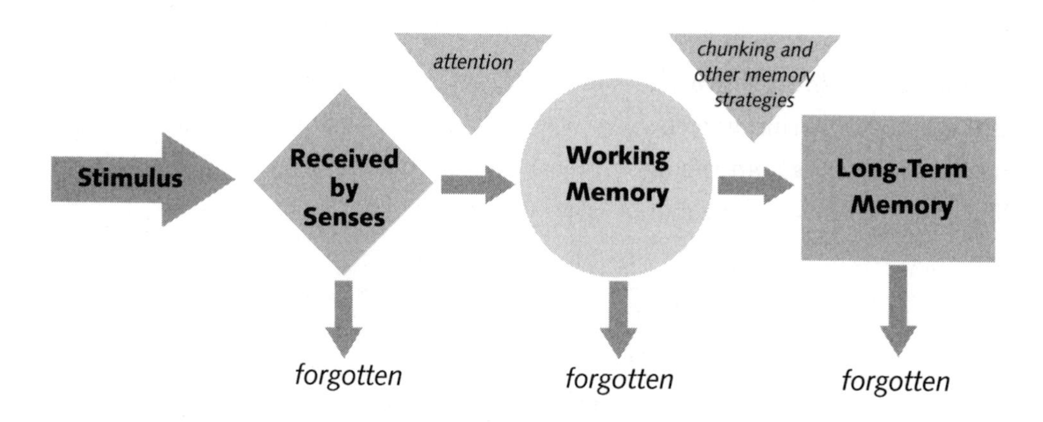

Our brains work fast. Let's backtrack for a moment to our discussion of the receptive stage of information processing. Incoming sensory information is only available for one to three seconds. We must move relevant information into our working memory or it is disregarded and lost. Our working memory has no longer than 30 seconds to decide what to do with this information. Any information that is not connected to a neural passageway built from our prior learning vanishes.

Thinking, as we know it, actually begins in the working memory. According to education theorists Feden and Vogel (2003), "Whatever we are conscious of at the moment is in our working memory. We can choose to either process it by connecting it with information in long-term memory, or we can just forget it" (p. 48). We must decide to either use this information or we will, quite literally, lose it.

There are many pieces of information that we choose to forget, such as a telephone number that we will only use once, or the vision of a dead animal lying in the road, or what we ate for breakfast the first Monday of March 2004. But if we don't want to forget something, how do we remember?

First, we have to focus on and pay attention to the information as it comes in; in other words, we have to be conscious of it. Cognitive theorists have found that our working memory can hold between five to nine pieces of information at any one time. We can use one of several techniques to get these bits of information transferred from our working memory into our long-term memory banks.

One technique is called chunking, which is defined as connecting pieces of related information together. Our most efficient students seek connections that relate pieces of information to one another. Feden and Vogel (2003) explain that chunking allows more information to be held in our working memory—if pieces "become chunks, then working memory can hold five to nine chunks of information, greatly increasing the amount of information that can be held, and manipulated, in working memory to work on cognitive tasks" (p. 49). For example, consider the word *car*. We know that a car is used for transportation; it has four wheels, seats, a front and a back, a steering wheel, a gas pedal, a brake pedal, an engine, and a muffler. The word *car* can conjure all of this information "chunked" together. The fact that we can chunk information together saves us a lot of space in our working memory.

In fact, visual chunking is the most effective way to remember information. This is why webbing and concept maps are effective teaching tools. They help students see how information is related, helping them chunk it and connect it to information they already have. Other examples of chunking include grouping—such as grouping states by their geographic location (Northeast, South, Southwest, Midwest, and Northwest)—and timelines. For instance, let's say we are teaching American history. It is helpful to see the big picture, the entire timeline, from 1492 to present. If in a given week we are talking about the Revolutionary War, we could see that the information that week is from 1776 to 1778. This way the students see where this "chunk" of information fits into the bigger picture.

Long-Term Memory

The good news is that there appears to be no limit to the amount of information our long-term memory can hold. For new information to truly be learned, it must transfer, and assimilate, into our long-term memory. As teachers, how do we help our students transfer new information from the working memory into the long-term memory? This transfer involves several processes. Let's look at how young students learn the letters of the alphabet. Each time students learn to recognize a new letter, a new neural passageway is formed between the eye and the occipital lobe; each time a new sound is learned, a path is formed from the ears to the temporal lobes. As these networks are activated repeatedly over time, a memory trace begins to form. When students are asked to look at the letter and hear the sound it represents, specific neural networks are joined together. James Zull (2002) states, "the knowledge in our minds consists of neural networks in our brains, so if that knowledge is to grow, the neural networks must physically change" (p. 112). Thus, students seeing an *a* and simultaneously saying "a" are wiring together two neural networks. With repetition, the networks become stronger and more efficient. In addition to repetition, there are metacognitive strategies that can be used to facilitate the transfer of information into long-term memory.

Metacognitive Memory Strategies. Metacognition is the ability to facilitate learning by taking control and directing our own thinking process. It is the ability to think about the way we learn. Janet Lerner (1993) states, "People exhibit metacognitive behavior when they do something to help themselves learn and remember, such as preparing shopping lists to remember what to buy, outlining difficult technical chapters to help understand and remember the material, or rehearsing and repeating what has just been learned to help stabilize and strengthen their learning" (p. 205). We can help our students learn more efficiently by teaching them strategies they can then apply independently.

Table 6.2 presents six strategies that will help information in the working memory form a memory trace and flow into our long-term memory. You can use these strategies in your teaching to help students better grasp and remember content. But also teach students the strategies themselves, so they can apply them to their own learning independently.

All of these strategies are important; however, I would like to give some special attention to the topic of reflection. I believe that we all need to take time each day to reflect on the complex aspects of our personal and professional life.

Time to Reflect

Before we can comprehend any new material in any real depth, we need time to reflect. As Zull (2002) states, "Reflection is a search for connections—literally!" (p.164). In other words, we need to give our brain time to find the right neural connections. As teachers, we actually need to

Table 6.2 Memory Strategies

Strategy	Description
1. Chunk information	Chunking entails finding a way to link two or more separate pieces of information together to form a greater whole. Chunking is an effective way to connect disparate neural passageways together in the brain; this process helps the brain to form a new superhighway.
2. Elaborate on content; make connections	Elaboration involves helping students make the connection between prior knowledge and new knowledge. This strategy helps students create networks of concepts that are linked together; these help create numerous neural connections.
3. Show or create visual images	Images give learners a visual perspective, allowing them to use their right brain along with their left brain. We can use images from pictures, books, and the Internet, and we can encourage students to make their own images.
4. Organize information	There are many ways that teachers can help students organize information. It is beneficial to give the big perspective first, and then fill in the details. Outlines are good for left-brain students; graphic organizers are best for right-brain students. Color cues help.
5. Incorporate repetition	When the same networks are activated over and over again, the memory trace becomes stronger. This leads to stronger neural roads.
6. Take time to reflect	In order to understand something in an in-depth manner, we need time to reflect. Both sleep, and pausing between learning events, are crucial in the formation of long-term memories.

structure "downtime" for our students to allow them to reflect. The making of a long-term memory requires chemical changes in the synapses. Our students' neural passageways need time to link prior knowledge and to create new synapses for long-term memory.

When we reflect, we use images, language, and sometimes movement. To reflect in an in-depth manner, most of us need to close out the incoming sensory stimuli. How can teachers provide reflection time for their students? Several suggestions are listed below.

1. After discussing a big concept in class, put students in pairs to discuss what they have just learned. Each student can present two ideas that they have learned. This process gives students time to synthesize what they've learned. When they synthesize, they strengthen neural passageways.
2. Give students five minutes to write down two big ideas that they have just learned. This activity will give the brain time to search for deeper connections.
3. Ask each student to write a question that he or she has about material they have just read. This activity will also provide time to reflect.

4. Ask students to close their eyes and breathe calmly for two minutes. Ask them to think about the concepts that they have just learned.

Adding time for reflection has become part of my lesson planning. I believe that it does indeed give students the ammunition they need to make new material "theirs." Zull (2002) considers reflection an instrumental step in learning: "The art of directing and supporting reflection is part of the art of changing a brain. It is the art of leading a student toward comprehension" (p. 164).

More Ways to Enhance Our Students' Memories

Below are two principles of brain-based learning that you can use to enhance your students' memory: Make connections through use of students' prior knowledge and help students find relevance, patterns, and meaning in course content.

Make Connections to Prior Knowledge

The literature on brain-based learning has a lot to say about making connections. One aspect of making new neural connections is associated with how the brain acquires knowledge—namely by linking prior knowledge to the new content that we are teaching (Caine, Caine, and Crowell, 1994). In other words, the more we can link students' previous knowledge and experiences with what we are currently teaching, the more the students will remember. Zull (2002) tells us that we are able to effectively teach our students new information only if we access their existing neural frameworks first.

Zull declares, "Prior knowledge is the beginning of new knowledge" (p. 93). He adds, "When we find out what our students already know, we are actually finding out about their neuronal networks. We are discovering the connections they have in their brains." When we introduce new information, we are adding new knowledge to what's already there. And as this new knowledge is added, so are new neural networks. Zull suggests that we can help students locate their existing neural networks by asking them, "What does this make you think of?"

This suggests that we should find out what students know, or believe that they know, and use this as a tool for teaching. According to Zull, "existing neuronal networks open the door to effective teaching" (pp. 101–102). Part of the challenge for teachers then, is to find ways to "combine the established networks, or parts of them, with new networks—to build new concepts using a mix of the old and the new" (p. 119).

For example, let's say you are planning to teach a fourth-grade lesson on how the Earth was formed. Since it is best to connect the new information you're teaching to the information students may already have, you need to find out what they already know. A favorite way of mine to do this is using an overhead projector to write down the students' comments. To begin, you might ask the students, "What do you already know about the planet Earth?" Let's assume that the students respond with "It has oceans and continents." You would enthusiastically write these comments down on the overhead. You ask what else they know about the Earth, and you get, "The Earth has rivers and mountains," and again, you would excitedly add these to the list on the overhead.

This prior information becomes the foundation for the geography lesson. The students are already excited because you are taking their prior knowledge seriously. They can relax because they see that they already know something about this lesson, and they now have the confidence to learn something new. From here you can successfully proceed to connect their prior knowledge to new knowledge by showing them where the oceans, continents, rivers, and mountains are located on the globe and then launch into a more abstract presentation of the "history of the Earth."

If we were to peek inside our students' brains, we could see new neural networks being formed and connecting to existing frameworks. Zull (2002) puts it this way: "It seems that every fact we know, every idea we understand, and every action we take has the form of a network of neurons in our brain" (p. 99).

Help Students Find Relevance, Patterns, and Meaning in Course Content

Brain researchers have found that the human mind is motivated to constantly search for meaning. The brain learns in patterns and looks for depth: "The more teachers can build bridges between content and human experience, the more meaningful and effective the learning experience will be" (Caine, Caine, and Crowell, 1999, p. 95).

To help students remember, it is useful to distinguish between teaching primarily surface knowledge as opposed to deep understanding. Surface knowledge consists mostly of facts and is learned through straightforward memorization (for example, the presidents of the United States, the 50 states, the capitals, and so on). It's easy to forget surface knowledge because it often is not connected to prior learning.

In contrast, deep understanding is acquired when students get a feeling for the meaning of an idea. Their learning is organized around what the students regard as deeply important (for example, when learning about the Earth we can study the environment and how to protect it in order to help future generations). As the name implies, "deep understanding" involves learning about a topic in an in-depth manner. The teacher makes connections to prior knowledge, and thus creates a solid neural network highway.

In educational psychology, learning with feeling is known as "hot cognition." Hot cognition consists of the motivational aspect of cognition that excites students at both cognitive and emotional levels. "Cold cognition" is learning where we think about an issue without considering the emotional aspects (Feden and Vogel, 2003; Zajonic, 1980). I have found that my students unequivocally respond better when I can convey emotion in both my voice (prosody) and in the content itself. I go out of my way to help my students find relevance in what we are studying. One sure way to help them see relevance is to use the emotions. This is, I believe, what my friend Mary Raddock does so well; she uses her emotions to convey meaning.

Lynn, a middle-school teacher, asked her students to read the play *A Raisin in the Sun* by Lorraine Hansberry. The play, which takes place in the 1950's, powerfully presents the struggles of an African-American family living in Chicago as they strive for the realization of their dreams. This teacher also brought in the CD, *Raisin*, to accompany the book. She was astonished at the emotional dimension that listening to the songs on the CD provided. The varying feelings in the songs, ranging from intense to gentle, conveyed an emotional intensity that the words alone could not provide.

How Do We Remember Without Memorizing?

Surely all of us remember having to memorize ad nauseam when we were students. I remember being annoyed at having to memorize vocabulary definitions with no context being given in which to remember them. The brain craves deep understanding. If we focus more on deep understanding, we are more likely to make connections with our students, and our students are more likely to make connections with the material. If we give students vocabulary words in the context of a specific area, they will be more likely to make the words their own.

For example, you could give your students vocabulary words in the context of a unit you are studying, such as the history of the Earth. Giving them a pictorial illustration labeled with the vocabulary words (for example, *glaciers, fossils, limestone, dinosaurs, mammoths,* and *granite*) will help the words become meaningful to the students. In this case, memory will be helped even more by creating a story with the class that uses the vocabulary words. Let the class make up the story as you write it on the chalkboard. Each child can copy the story on his or her paper. That way, they get the experience of spelling the words, but also of seeing them in context. The fact that they make the words their own greatly increases the likelihood they will remember the words at a deep level, rather than simply memorizing them for a test on Friday afternoon, only to forget half of them by Friday night.

For another example, let's consider the geography lesson I described earlier. It might be tempting to give the students too much surface knowledge by presenting the three eras (Paleozoic, Mesozoic, and Cenozoic), plus each of the periods inside each area (each era has between three and seven periods). So much surface knowledge (facts only) is likely to overwhelm students.

Instead, you could appeal to deep understanding by presenting an overview of the Earth's history and how geologists study rocks and fossils to determine the evolution of life on our planet. To make the learning relevant to the students' lives, you could divide the class into three groups, with each group being in charge of an era. Each group could be responsible for presenting specific data to the class about their era, such as what creatures evolved during their era, what the Earth looked like, how the Earth changed, and so on. To ensure that students retained information from the eras that were not their own, you could ask each group to write a brief, nongraded quiz for the rest of the class to take.

Remember, the big idea behind deep understanding is to get students fired up about something, to get them excited, so that they make what they've learned their own. When students demonstrate that they're excited about their lessons, you can be sure their neurons are actively firing.

The neural superhighways in our brain represent the information we have learned over and over again, and now know automatically. For most adults, "automatic activities" are represented in our abilities to read without decoding, and to drive without thinking about the mechanics of driving. The making of neural connections and superhighways in the brain is at the heart of teaching and learning.

Expressing Information

The third, and final stage in the learning loop is the expressive or output. Output represents the physical part of how we learn. Examples include writing, speaking, gardening, playing the piano, and playing sports. Output is the only part of information processing that we can actually see and measure without the use of brain scans.

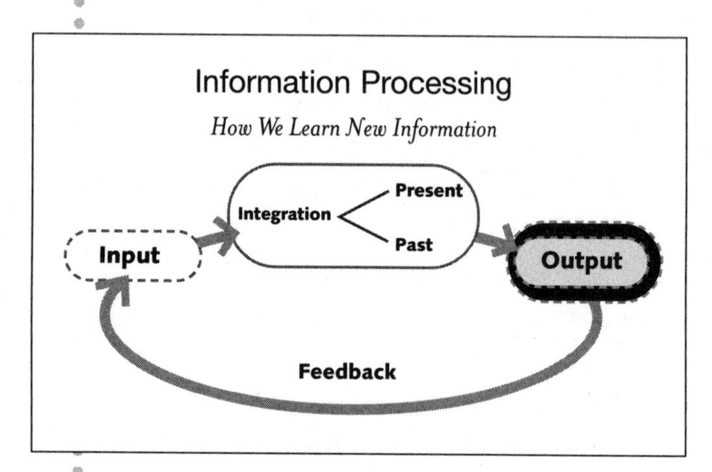

Kephart (1971) defines output as "a pattern of neural impulses which the brain sends down to the muscles, and results in movement" (p. 112). Movement comprises two areas, fine and gross motor development. Gross motor movement develops first in infants. Over time, our gross motor development goes from sitting, crawling, walking, hopping, skipping, throwing a ball, and riding a bicycle, to more coordinated activities including skateboarding, roller blading, gymnastics, skiing, martial arts, swimming, and playing team sports.

Our fine motor development begins a bit later. Fine motor development includes the coordination of our eyes and hands and our vocal chords. Some examples of eye-and-hand coordination include eating with our fingers, using a spoon to eat, assembling puzzles, creating with Legos, cutting and pasting, sewing, writing, drawing, and keyboarding. Examples of our vocal chord coordination include cooing, laughing, humming, speaking one word, speaking in sentences, shouting, and singing.

Our gross and fine motor coordination represent the different types of movement we're capable of. But what is the relationship between our brain and our ability to move? Are they separate or are they interconnected? The next section discusses the interaction between the brain and the body.

Mind and Body

Carla Hannaford (1995) states that "movement is an indispensable part of learning and thinking" (p.107). Over the past 150 years, there have been many scholars who have shunned the notion that the brain is responsible for the movements of our body. Many believed that the cerebral cortex was the location of the mind alone and had no relationship to movement (or emotion). Today, many people still believe that the mind and the body are entirely separate entities.

These people might be surprised to know that, like emotion, our ability to move originates in the brain. In fact, there are areas of the brain specifically associated with muscle movement, including the cerebellum (part of the reptilian brain) and the basal ganglia (part of the limbic system).

In Hannaford's book *Smart Moves: Why Learning Is Not All in Your Head*, she demonstrates ways in which our mind and body interconnect with our experiences in the environment. For example, when students of all ages sit for too long, we often see them slump down in their chairs. This posture is a clear indication that the brain is not getting enough oxygen and blood to maintain alertness. Interestingly, when we stand up and move, our heart rate increases; this results in more oxygen and blood flowing to the brain. The extra blood and oxygen helps to increase neural firing. Movement in the classroom enhances learning.

In fact, there have been many studies that relate exercise to improved overall mental health (Dryfoos, 2000; Lambert, 2000; Hannaford, 1995). Exercise has been found to trigger the release of BDNF, a brain-derived neurotropic factor. BDNF enhances learning by enhancing the ability of neurons to communicate. Those who exercise regularly have been found to have quicker reaction times, more energy, creativity, and higher test scores.

Eric Jensen (2000) notes, "Brain-compatible learning means weaving math, movement, geography, social skills, role-playing, science, and physical education together" (p. 167). Of course, using movement when we teach brings Gardner's bodily-kinesthetic intelligence alive in the classroom as well.

Closing the Learning Loop

As we mentioned in the first part of this chapter our brain and our body are considered a "closed system," indicating that the cycle of learning is continuous. The learning process is a continuous loop: Output frequently becomes input. For example, a first-grade teacher asks her student, Sam, to come to the chalkboard and write his name. In the first pass-through of the learning loop, Sam hears and processes the request; consequently he gets up and comes to the board. In the second pass-through of the learning loop, Sam picks up the chalk and writes his name. Let's say that he writes the S in his name backward. On the third pass-through of the learning loop, Sam checks his work and sees his error; in this case, the visual-motor output becomes visual input. Sam's brain processes the fine motor output as incorrect. In the fourth loop, Sam erases the backward S and writes it correctly. He looks, processes the fact that the letters in his name are correct, and sits down.

This scenario demonstrates how output becomes input. And, Sam has just strengthened a neural passageway (that connects to many other parts of his brain).

Looking Ahead

We have completed our exploration of the information processing cycle. We can use these three stages—receptive, processing, and expressive—to formulate a definition of learning: Learning is the ability to extract relevant sensory information from the environment, process this information in the working memory, integrate the information into our long-term memory, and act on this information in terms of relevant motor responses.

In the following chapter, I'll connect this information processing theory to our learning style practices.

Chapter 7

Learning Styles

"Name anything that humans can know, think, feel, or do, and we can find a part of the brain, or a combination of parts, that specializes in that thing.""

—James Zull (2002, p. 100)

As we saw in Chapter Six, information is continuously flowing—input is received, processed, and ultimately expressed. In this chapter we will use our knowledge of information processing as a foundation on which to build an understanding of learning styles, which describe a person's preference for how to receive, process, and express information. The three primary learning styles are auditory, visual, and tactile-kinesthetic, and each uses a different part of the brain (Jensen, 1995).

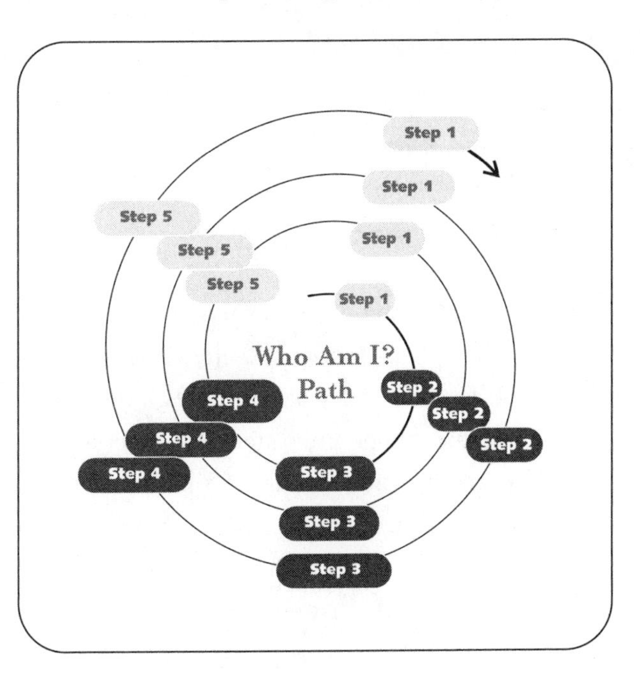

In the first part of this chapter, you'll find questionnaires to help you determine your own learning style, the third step on the "Who Am I?" path of discovery. Later in the chapter is a questionnaire for students to take to identify their own learning styles. The chapter concludes with teaching strategies and learning activities suited to each learning style.

What Is My Receptive Learning Style?

Although we use all of our seven sensory modalities to learn (see page 103), most of us have a preference for how we receive incoming sensory information. Are we visually, auditorily, or kinesthetically inclined?

Which of your senses do you rely upon most to teach and to learn? The learning style questionnaire on pages 120–121 was designed with teachers in mind. Answer the questions and follow the scoring directions to determine whether you teach and learn through a primary modality.

What Is My Processing Learning Style?

Think for a moment about how you prefer to process new information. Is it in a left-brain, sequential manner or a right-brain, random manner? Or perhaps both? In the graduate classes I teach, students identify and discuss their strengths and weaknesses with both an oral presentation and a paper that addresses the "Who Am I?" inquiry.

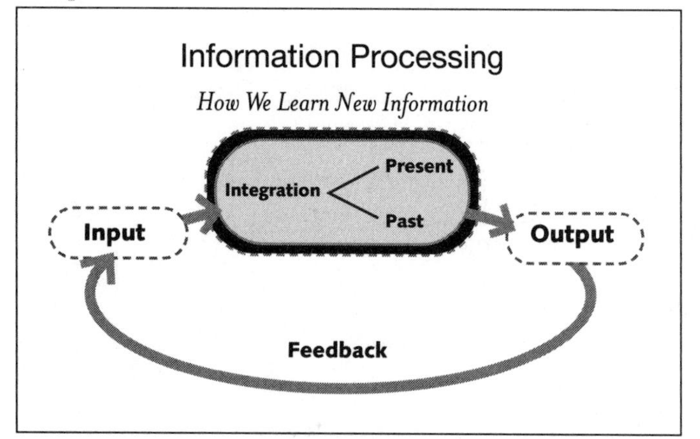

People with right-brain tendencies often process information in a random manner. Several of my right-brain graduate students (all teachers) have described this random process both through their writing and in their "Who Am I?" presentations. One student, Sandy, had a coteacher observe and record her actions for 10 minutes. Sandy's goal was to write a learning objective for a student with learning disabilities. Here's what the coteacher observed: Sandy sat down at her cluttered desk and started to write for one and a half minutes. Then she got up, erased the chalkboard, sat down and straightened her desk. She continued to write for one minute, then got up and rearranged a bulletin board, then sat down and listened to a voice mail message. She then finished the learning objective.

So what happened here? Sandy's attention went to many other things during the time that she was "writing the learning objective." She explained to me that this is how she always is, that she always multitasks, and things always get done. Sandy's work is accomplished in a random manner.

In contrast, Donna, a sixth-grade science teacher, is left-brained. Her "Who Am I?" presentation to the class was organized with a handout packet and an accompanying PowerPoint presentation. Her oral presentation was designed to follow the slides in her PowerPoint sequence. She had also written a poem to represent her family life; she gave a copy of this poem to all of us.

Donna was dressed in a business suit. She told the class that her bedroom and kitchen closets were always kept neat and organized. She uses a "master schedule" that allows her to coordinate her time demands with those of each member in the family.

Mike is middle-brained. He is, perhaps, a tad more flexible in his teaching and his life than either right-brained Sandy or left-brained Donna. Mike feels there are many things he can do well. He plays the trumpet and coaches girls' hockey. He teaches high school algebra. Mike reports being sequential when he teaches math as he puts outlines on the chalkboard and keeps an "orderly" classroom. He reports being random when he plays the trumpet; he will play according to the mood he is currently feeling.

Mike was truly middle-brained during his "Who Am I?" presentation. He explained that he teaches in a left-brain sequential manner; he gave all of us a sample of an algebra lecture, followed by problems to solve. He then treated us to some trumpet music, which expressed how he was currently feeling: "stressed."

The Processing Learning Style Questionnaire on page 122 is designed to help you identify how you process information. Do these answers correspond to your answers on the Alert Scale? On the Alert Scale you found out if you are a left-, right-, or middle-brain learner and teacher. You are likely to find that your score on the Processing Learning Style Questionnaire correlates with your score on the Alert Scale.

Examining your learning style through questionnaires such as those provided in this book or other commercial ones is only one way to look at how we process information; however, our brain is far more complicated than this one method indicates. Our brain processes information from all seven of our senses simultaneously. Some of the other ways to look at learning styles include abstract versus concrete, multitask versus single-task, introvert versus extrovert, and thinkers versus feelers.

What Is My Expressive Learning Style?

The third area in the learning loop constitutes the way we prefer to express ourselves. Writing, drawing, speaking, and performing are all ways we can communicate with others. The following questionnaire was designed to help you examine your expressive learning style(s). Are you primarily a talker, a writer, a thinker, a creator, a mover, or combination of these?

Receptive Learning Style Questionnaire for Teachers

Choose one phrase that best completes the sentence.

1. The way I prefer to teach during most of the day is
   ______ through explanation and discussion. (A)
   ______ with visual maps, models, movies, and group work. (V)
   ______ through the use of hands-on projects. (K)

2. The classroom atmosphere that I like to create the most is one of
   ______ curiosity, challenge, seriousness, and structure. (A)
   ______ creative activity using varying materials; stimulating activities. (V)
   ______ cooperation and collaboration between groups of students. (K)

3. The best way for me to remember specific information is to
   ______ listen to a speaker, and repeat it to myself. (A)
   ______ see it. (V)
   ______ write it down. (K)

4. The best way for me to remember large chunks of information is to
   ______ listen with concentration. (A)
   ______ make creative visual maps. (V)
   ______ tap the information to a beat or walk around. (K)

5. Teaching strategies that I like to incorporate the most are
   ______ short lectures, discussion, and creative writing. (A)
   ______ creating projects related to subject matter. (V)
   ______ hands-on demonstrations and role-playing. (K)

6. I am happiest when my lessons are based on
   ______ major themes and inquiry. (A)
   ______ the feelings and needs of my students. (V)
   ______ project work. (K)

7. The best way for me to remember something is to
   ______ listen carefully and ask for feedback. (A)
   ______ picture the message in my mind. (V)
   ______ move around while I listen and/or think about the information. (K)

8. If I am trying to put something together for the first time, I

__✓__ read the manual and talk to myself as I assemble. (A)

______ read directions and visualize how the parts will go together. (V)

______ put the pieces together, then read the manual later. (K)

9. I like to listen to presenters who

__✓__ talk to the audience with passion. (A)

______ use PowerPoint slides or overheads while they talk. (V)

______ have the audience frequently get into groups or pairs. (K)

10. When I read a novel, I usually

______ analyze the plot and characters as I go along. (A)

__✓__ visualize the plot and characters; it's like watching a movie. (V)

______ try to feel the plot and characters, read for short periods of time. (K)

11. When I have to get to an important new place for an appointment, I want

______ to have precise written instructions. (A)

______ a clear map. (V)

__✓__ to actually drive there first, so I'll know how to get there for the appointment. (K)

12. When I meet new people, I will remember

______ what they said to me. (A)

______ what they looked like and what they wore. (V)

__✓__ how they acted toward me. (K)

Scoring—Count up the number of responses you had for each A, V, and K. Record your scores below.

__3__ = As (auditory responses)

__4__ = Vs (visual responses)

__5__ = Ks (kinesthetic responses)

It is possible to have one strong preference, two equal preferences, or to be almost evenly split between all three areas.

Processing Learning Style Questionnaire for Teachers

Please circle one answer for each item.

1. In my free time I would rather do (most of) the following
   (a) read, write, go on the computer, complete a crossword puzzle, do martial arts, play tennis
   (b) design curtains for the den, assemble a 500-piece jigsaw puzzle, sew or knit, build a table out of wood, play volleyball, paint

2. I prefer a one-hour workshop speaker to
   (a) speak clearly to the audience for the full hour, using a PowerPoint presentation.
   (b) speak for 10 minutes, then divide the audience into small groups for activities.

3. When I set out to complete a task (such as planning a lesson), I usually
   (a) complete it, then go on to something else.
   (b) do several things simultaneously.

4. When I read a novel,
   (a) I see a few pictures in my head, but I mostly read the words and think about what I am reading.
   (b) I get continual pictures in my head, it's like watching a movie.

5. When I am driving home from a new restaurant 10 miles from where I live,
   (a) I need accurate directions to get back home or I am likely to get lost.
   (b) I can just reverse the directions spatially in my mind, and get home with no problem.

Scoring

If you circled 4–5 a's you have more of a sequential (left-brain) processing style.

If you circled 4–5 b's, you have more of a random (right-brain) processing style.

If you circled a combination of 2 a's and 3 b's, or 3 a's and 2 b's, you are a middle-brain learner, using both random and sequential processing styles depending on the situation.

Expressive Learning Style Questionnaire for Teachers

Please check one for each pair.

Given the choice, I would rather

______ dance in front of others. (M)
__✓__ speak in front of others. (T)

__✓__ write an essay. (W)
______ make pottery. (C)

______ discuss and debate politics. (T)
__✓__ write a four-page paper. (W)

______ illustrate a children's book. (C)
__✓__ write a children's book. (W)

______ climb a small mountain. (M)
__✓__ write a poem. (W)

__✓__ take an exercise class. (M)
______ take a watercolor class. (C)

______ design a new shirt. (C)
__✓__ attend a conference for teachers. (Th)

______ make a flower garden. (M)
__✓__ play a musical instrument. (C)

__✓__ read a novel. (Th)
______ write an editorial for the newspaper. (W)

______ wash my car. (M)
__✓__ read a mystery. (Th)

__✓__ teach a language arts class. (T)
______ teach an art class. (C)

__✓__ read a nonfiction book. (Th)
______ do needlepoint or crocheting. (C)

______ be part of a listserv that discusses and analyzes selected poets. (Th)
__✓__ e-mail and Instant Message friends. (W)

__✓__ teach a creative writing class. (W)
______ teach woodworking. (C)

__✓__ read a chapter book out loud to my students. (T)
______ supervise a hands-on project with students. (M)

______ play tennis. (M)

__✓__ sing in a choir. (C)

__✓__ speak to a small group about a topic I enjoy. (T)

______ write an eight-page paper for graduate school. (W)

______ swim. (M)

__✓__ present a workshop. (T)

__✓__ research a topic on the computer. (Th)

______ write lyrics to a song. (W)

__✓__ sponsor the school newspaper. (W)

______ attend a lecture and discussion series. (Th)

______ play basketball. (M)

__✓__ talk to a friend for two hours on the telephone. (T)

______ write a short story. (W)

__✓__ take and learn from a psychological questionnaire. (Th)

__✓__ be part of a book club. (Th)

______ be part of an exercise class. (M)

__✓__ help start a psychology-type club. (Th)

______ direct a school play. (T)

__✓__ talk to a friend over coffee. (T)

______ take piano lessons. (C)

Scoring—*Tally your response for each category and record the totals here.*

undeveloped __1__ = Ms (movement responses)

undeveloped __0__ = Cs (creative responses)

mod __6__ = Ws (writing responses)

mod __5__ = Ths (thinking responses)

strong __8__ = Ts (talking responses)

You can score up to 10 in each category.

A score of 7–10 indicates a strong output area for you.

A score of 4–6 indicates a moderate output area for you.

A score of 0–3 indicates an undeveloped output area for you.

Putting It All Together

You have now analyzed your learning style from the three information processing perspectives: receptive, processing, and expressive. Fill in the profile below so that you have your "Information Processing Picture" all in one spot.

My Complete Learning Style Profile

1. **My receptive learning style is . . .**
   (Auditory, Visual, Kinesthetic)

2. **My processing learning style is . . . *(Left, Right, Middle)***

3. **My expressive learning style(s) is/are . . .**
   (Movement, Creative, Writing, Thinking, Talking)

4. **Reflection:**

Our Students' Learning Styles

Incorporating teaching strategies that appeal to different learning styles is one more way to create a successful brain-based learning classroom. It is not difficult to teach to our students' strongest modalities during at least part of the day. If we alternate between visual, auditory, and tactile-kinesthetic learning activities, we will cover all our bases.

On page 127 is a questionnaire that you can copy and give to your students in order to help them determine their preferred learning style. It will also give you a read on your class. If most students in a particular group are visual learners, you can incorporate teaching strategies that engage them in nearly every lesson. If you have just a few tactile-kinesthetic learners, you can ensure there's always a choice activity to appeal to them for independent work or homework while occasionally incorporating whole-class tactile-kinesthetic activities.

It is okay to read it to them out loud in a group setting and have them circle their answers; or you can read it to them individually, and help them write down their choice on the answers.

Talking With Students About Their Results

Once the questionnaire is complete, explain the different learning styles and emphasize that one is not better than another. It's simply a brain preference. During the discussion, help students see that their hobbies are often connected with their learning-style preference. For example, a visual learner is likely to have hobbies building 3-D puzzles, assembling car kits, using Legos, singing, painting, sewing, and so on. Understanding the correlation between their learning-style strength and their hobbies helps them make a connection. In addition, you can share study strategies and learning activities that allow students to use their preferences. Use the lists on pages 129–131 to get started.

Creating Visual, Auditory, and Kinesthetic Experiences in the Classroom

There are good reasons to teach using different learning styles. Consider this observation from Eric Jensen (1996), "Many learners who seem apathetic would be very enthusiastic if the learning was offered in their preferred style. There are many ways to learn, so provide continual variety and expose them to many other styles so that they may become flexible learners. Create options for your learners so that they can learn in the style of their choice" (p. 140).

> "The most important key to learning-style effectiveness is providing choice and a variety of methods for students to learn."
>
> — *Eric Jensen*

There are only three learning modalities to consider when we plan our lessons. It is reasonably easy to create visual, auditory, and kinesthetic activities for our students. Some specific examples of teaching strategies are included on page 134.

How Do You Learn Best?

The Children's Learning Style Questionnaire

Please read each statement and circle the answer that seems the most like you.

1. How do you like to learn something new?
   (a) By listening to my teacher tell me about it first.
   (b) By watching my teacher do it first.
   (c) By doing it myself first.

2. What would you like to do most in your free time indoors?
   (a) Read a fun book, comic book, or magazine
   (b) Paint, color, draw, or sketch.
   (c) Build with Legos or blocks or dance.

3. What would you like to do most on the weekends?
   (a) Talk on the phone with my friends or IM friends.
   (b) Play a musical instrument, do artwork, or listen to music.
   (c) Play sports.

4. What is the best way for you to remember a telephone number?
   (a) Say the numbers out loud over and over as I dial.
   (b) Picture the numbers in my head.
   (c) Write all of the numbers in the air.

5. What do you like the most when you see a movie?
   (a) What the main characters say to each other.
   (b) The clothes they wear, the scenery, and the special effects.
   (c) How I feel during the movie (happy, scared, mad).

6. When you read a story, which of the following happens?
   (a) I think about the meaning of the words.
   (b) I see pictures in my mind about what I am reading.
   (c) I feel what the characters are feeling.

7. How would you prefer to describe an "unusual animal" to someone?
   (a) Explain the animal in words.
   (b) Draw a picture of the animal.
   (c) Use my body to imitate the animal.

8. I understand something best after I
   (a) think about it.
   (b) see it.
   (c) try it out.

9. One of my favorite ways to spend time is
   (a) listening to music.
   (b) playing video games on the computer.
   (c) going shopping.

10. When I meet someone new, I will mostly remember
   (a) what he or she said.
   (b) what he or she was wearing.
   (c) how he or she acted, or how I felt.

Scoring—*Add up all of your points in each category; record your scores here.*

______ a's (auditory learner)

______ b's (visual learner)

______ c's (kinesthetic learner)

Some people will have a strongest way to learn, some will have two ways that are almost equally strong, and others will be able to learn using all three ways. Which one were you?

Learning by Hearing

Strategies for Auditory Learners

1. When doing reading response, try to write and speak about your responses, as these tend to be your strongest ways to communicate.
2. Read important passages in a book out loud, as hearing it will help you remember the content.
3. Listen to books on tape and take notes as you go along.
4. Listen to a program on talk radio, and give your assessment of it.
5. Listen carefully when others are talking in order to enhance your communication skills.
6. Speak often with others in order to clarify ideas in your own mind.
7. When you come across a new word that you do not know, try and sound it out.
8. Volunteer to be in a debate.
9. In group activities, volunteer to be the presenter, or the narrator.
10. When giving directions to others, give them out loud instead of writing them down.
11. When listening to music, try to listen separately for the lyrics versus the music.
12. When studying, try and find a quiet spot so that you will not be distracted.
13. If you have to memorize something, try and remember it step by step, or in a sequential manner.
14. Use words thoughtfully to describe to others how you are feeling.
15. Listen to people's tones of voice in order to gain understanding of what they are feeling.
16. Put poems that you have written to music, and listen for the beat in conjunction with the words of the poems.

Learning by Seeing

Strategies for Visual Learners

1. When doing literature responses, opt to draw or create images that express your response, as these tend to be your strongest way to communicate.
2. In group activities, volunteer to be the artist or illustrator.
3. When giving directions to others, write them down by creating a map.
4. When studying, use crayons, colored pencils, or colored markers to underscore important points.
5. When reading, carefully observe the maps and graphs to give you information.
6. When studying, be aware of the visual images in your mind, these will help you with long-term memory.
7. Watch people's expressions carefully in order to gain understanding of their feelings.
8. Make cartoons, or a series of cartoons, to illustrate your feelings or perceptions.
9. Make graphs or pictures to illustrate what you have read; the pictures will help you remember.
10. Use Cuisenaire Rods and other manipulatives to help you learn new math concepts.
11. Illustrate book reports and other written projects.
12. Learn computer graphics and create PowerPoint presentations.

Learning by Doing

Strategies for Kinesthetic Learners

1. When doing literature response, opt to act out or dramatize your response, as learning by doing and moving tends to be your strongest way to communicate.
2. When listening to a teacher, always take notes, as writing will help enhance your memory of what was presented.
3. Be aware of what you are feeling in your "gut," this will help you communicate with others.
4. Taking frequent breaks when you are studying will prevent you from getting restless.
5. When doing activities in groups, volunteer to be the one who performs the demonstrations (such as the way ancient Greeks used to dress).
6. When given the choice on how to complete assignments, chose to make things such as mobiles, dioramas, posters, etc.
7. When trying to memorize, walk around and say the words out loud. The physical activity will help you remember.
8. Volunteer to role-play key characters in books and other roles in the class.
9. Put on a puppet show to demonstrate your understanding of content.
10. Use blocks and manipulatives to master math concepts.
11. Use software such as *Shufflepuck Café*, an eye-hand coordination game, or *Flight Simulator*, a motion-simulation game.
12. Dress up as a character from the 1800s to demonstrate your understanding of United States history.
13. Volunteer to choreograph a scene from a play.
14. Take pictures or video recordings for specific assignments.
15. Watch people's body language in order to gain understanding of what they are feeling.

Teaching Visual Learners

Visual learners have difficulty absorbing information through verbal presentations, no matter how interesting the presentation may be. Their receptive strength is visual, so providing visual aids to go along with the oral presentation helps them immensely.

I have found it extremely beneficial to add handouts, overheads, PowerPoint slides, and humorous cartoons to my presentations. I often draw concept maps on the board to connect major ideas visually. You may also wish to include charts, posters, and computer software. Since visual learners can learn by seeing, they can easily remember the shapes of graphic organizers, graphs, and maps. In addition, using color is a wonderful way to help a visual learner to remember. You can color code overheads or charts and teach students to use colored markers to highlight main ideas, vocabulary words, and so on.

Visual learners are often able to draw the concepts you present orally. It is a good idea to let students draw while you are lecturing, encouraging them to focus their drawings on concepts contained in your presentations.

Teaching Auditory Learners

Auditory learners love a good lecture and discussion! A stimulated adult auditory learner can listen to an informed teacher speak for hours. From an information-processing perspective, their receptive strength is auditory; they enjoy listening to words. Their expressive strengths are often oral and written expression. They tend to be effective communicators.

This group constitutes our "traditional" learners. Most prefer a quiet classroom with desks lined up in rows. Auditory learners like to concentrate on one thing at a time. They are easily distracted by too much visual and auditory noise. They do not like an exorbitant amount of group work and hands-on projects.

It is helpful for auditory learners to work on assignments with one or two other students, because such an interchange encourages them to talk about the information, and hear it as well. Other strategies include listening to books on tape, and taping ideas that they want to remember. Finally, it is beneficial for auditory learners to use their auditory strengths in their assignments; many auditory learners are good speakers as well. You might consider letting them orally present some of their assignments.

Teaching Kinesthetic Learners

The two most important things to remember about kinesthetic learners are that they need to move frequently throughout the day, and they learn best with hands-on activities. Of the three learning style groups, sitting still and listening is the hardest for kinesthetic learners. In fact, most kinesthetic learners would rather move than read.

Physically, these students use their bodies a lot. They tend to talk with their hands; they respond better to a congratulatory handshake than to a verbal compliment. These are the students to send on errands for you—they will appreciate the movement and the break from sitting.

Kinesthetic learners are avid note takers—after all, they learn by using their body. In fact you may find them moving their body as they learn (shaking a leg, playing with their hair, and so on). Typically, these students excel in sports, dance, cheerleading, scouts, and theater. In the classroom, they enjoy role-playing and performing; anything with movement in it will help them learn. To appeal to them, you might try letting students "act out" the punctuation marks they encounter (students might jump up when they see an exclamation point, get up and stretch when they see a period, and so on.) This type of activity will help kinesthetic learners master the content, and give them the physical break they need.

Performing in school or community plays provides a great opportunity for students to immerse themselves in a theme and learn it in a profound way. But what about the classroom? Let's say you are teaching American history. Encouraging students to inhabit the persona of historical figures will give kinesthetic students a perfect way to get information into their long-term memory. If a student "becomes" Abraham Lincoln and performs a soliloquy about whether or not to go to war, you can be sure the desired content will get into her long-term memory.

In language arts, letting a student role-play his favorite literary figure will give him confidence in what he has read. It will allow him to have a deeper appreciation of the book. He will have to go over his lines time and time again. Remember, repetition is a strategy that gets information into the long-term memory.

Jensen (2000) suggests that teachers should try to "associate new learning with various physical movements" (p.173). He recommends having students move around the room in a fashion similar to a scavenger hunt. Some examples include having students get up and touch round objects, touch blue objects, or touch two things that begin with the letter *d*. In math you could have students act out equations. Make two groups of students and ask the class to add up the total number; volunteers can come up and represent the sum. With a little creativity, tactile-kinesthetic activities can be incorporated into any subject area.

Auditory

- *Lecture*
- *Read aloud*
- *Focus on phonics*
- *Lead discussions*
- *Allow small-group discussions*
- *Hold sharing sessions at the end of lessons (students share verbally what they accomplished during a work session)*
- *Hold debates*
- *Assign oral presentations*
- *Assign recitations (poetry, speeches)*
- *Play music related to theme*
- *Listen for beats and rhythms*
- *Play recordings of speeches*
- *Let students teach each other in pairs*

Visual

- *Use graphic organizers*
- *Incorporate overheads and PowerPoint slides into lectures*
- *Provide handouts to accompany lectures so students can read along*
- *Show maps*
- *Teach visual imagery*
- *Use graphs and charts to represent data*
- *Show movies and news clips*
- *Allow students to respond through drawings (with accompanying written description/summary)*
- *Assign posters and illustrations to accompany presentations and reports*
- *Provide written copies of speeches, lyrics, poems*
- *Use color codes*

Tactile-Kinesthetic

- *Allow students to role-play*
- *Assign performances of poems, speeches, songs*
- *Provide manipulatives whenever possible, not only in math*
- *Get in touch with feelings and gut reactions*
- *Bring in artifacts (such as fossils, clothing related to historical period, etc.)*
- *Offer foods related to theme (depending on age, students can prepare and bring in)*
- *Assign models and dioramas to accompany presentations and reports*
- *Assign plays for students to perform or read aloud (Readers Theater)*
- *Schedule field trips*
- *Teach note-taking strategies*
- *Incorporate dance*
- *Take pictures to illustrate projects*

Teaching Suggestions Using Learning Styles

Use the following checklist to spark ideas for incorporating activities matched to different learning styles in your lessons. Offering choice is key. For example, if you are doing a poetry unit and you want everyone to read and share a favorite poem, you can offer options that appeal to each of the learning styles. Auditory learners can recite the poem for the class. Visual learners can illustrate the poem and present it to a small group. Tactile-kinesthetic learners could act out the poem for a small group or the class. Each option fulfills your objective while allowing students the opportunity to demonstrate their learning through their strengths.

Learning Styles in Action

The following is an integrated science and language arts lesson developed to incorporate activities for each learning style.

Topic: Thunder and Lightning
Grades 2, 3, 4

Objectives:

Science Objectives—Earth Science: Thunder and Lightning

1. To define thunder and lightning
2. To discuss thunder and lightning from a historical perspective
3. To identify the different sounds of thunder
4. To learn the cause of thunder and lightning
5. To learn how to count the number of seconds between when the lightning flashes and the thunder roars; this number is approximately the distance of the storm in miles
6. To learn how lightning is caused
7. To identify the four forms of lightning: forked, streak, ribbon, and chain

Reading Objectives:

1. Read *Thunder Cake* by Patricia Polacco in class with teacher
2. Read *Otherwise Known as Sheila the Great* by Judy Blume individually.
3. Look up thunder and lightning using Web quests on the Internet.

Integration Objectives:

1. To synthesize information red on thunder and lightning from books and the Internet Web quests
2. To learn to recognize that everyone has fears
3. To learn ways to conquer fears

Materials Needed:

1. Books: *Thunder Cake* by Patricia Polacco and *Otherwise Known as Sheila the Great* by Judy Blume
2. A previously made (or bought) thunder cake and milk or juice
3. A Xeroxed copy of the thunder cake recipe from Polacco's book
4. A CD player and the CD *The King and I*
5. Typed words for each student to the song "Whistle a Happy Tune"
6. Paper bags to simulate thunder
7. Flashlights to simulate lightning
8. Computers with access to the Internet to conduct a Web quest on thunder and lightning

1. Auditory Activities

a. Students engage in a discussion with teacher about being frightened by storms and other things such as spiders, the dark, clowns, and dogs.
b. Students discuss new vocabulary words from the book *Thunder Cake* (*sultry, cooed, samovar*).
c. Students listen to the teacher read the story *Thunder Cake* by Patricia Polacco.
d. Students discuss relevant themes from the book regarding ways to master one's fear of storms.
e. Students listen to a direct teaching lesson on thunder and lightning.
f. Students engage in discussion of thunder and lightning.
g. Students read aloud the words to the song "Whenever I Feel Afraid" from *The King and I*.

2. Visual Activities

a. Students see pictures in the book *Thunder Cake*
b. Students read *Otherwise Known as Sheila the Great* by Judy Blume
c. Students see a simulated demonstration of thunder and lightning, and count the number of seconds between the lightning and the thunder.

3. Kinesthetic Activities

a. Students eat some Thunder Cake (chocolate cake, chocolate icing, with yellow thunderbolts).
b. Students listen to the lyrics in the song "Whenever I Feel Afraid" from the *King and I* and then sing it.
c. Students act out thunder and lightning.

4. Combined Auditory, Visual, and Kinesthetic Activities

a. Students discuss their fears in groups of four, and then write down their fears.

b. Students write ways to overcome the fear.

c. Students make a poster illustrating the fears and ways to overcome them.

d. Students in each group present their fears and poster to the rest of the class.

Setting Teaching Goals

The following mirror allows you to identify specific ways to incorporate diverse learning styles into your daily lesson plans. Use the lists on page 134 for ideas. As we have seen, it is important to take time to reflect. Taking the time to fill in the following page will help you incorporate the concept of learning styles into your long-term memory, and into your long-term teaching as well.

Looking Ahead

In the next chapter, we will examine the "Who Am I?" question from the affective perspective, as we take a closer look at our emotions and how they affect our teaching.

Who Am I?

Learning Styles Teaching Mirror and Goals

Since I am a ______________________________ learner,

I mostly teach in a ______________________________ manner.

I can teach my students with visual learning styles by adding

____

and ______________________________

to my ______________________________ lesson.

I can teach my students with auditory learning styles by adding

____

and ______________________________

to my ______________________________ lesson.

I can teach my students who are kinesthetic learners by adding

____

and ______________________________

to my ______________________________ lesson.

Chapter 8

Our Emotional Brain

"Do you put your learners' emotions and feelings on par with the mastery of content and skill learning? Remember, the two are directly biologically linked."

—Eric Jensen (2000, p. 201)

At least since the time of the ancient Greeks, a good many intelligent, thinking people have rejected the ideas that emotions were located in the brain or that feelings were separate from thought. Over the centuries, intellectual battles have been fought over which should guide human decision-making, thinking or feeling, the head or the heart. Most often, feeling has been considered subordinate. Historically, emotions have been "equated with sins and temptations to resist by reason and willpower" (LeDoux, 1996, p. 24). Or as Horace Walpole put it, "Life is a comedy for those who think and a tragedy for those who feel."

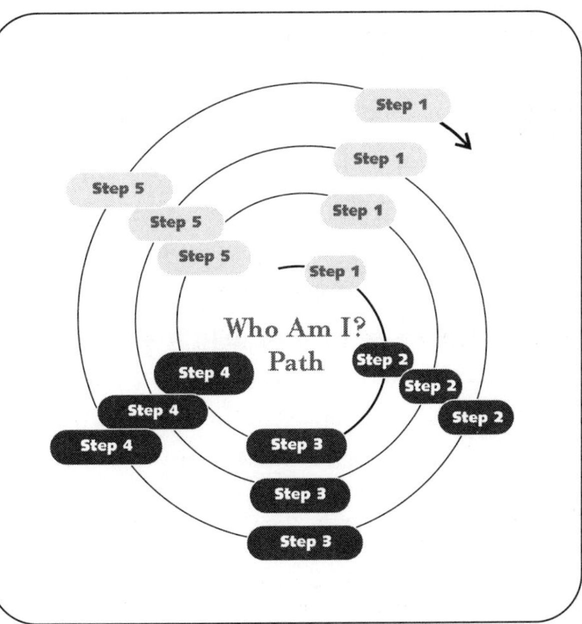

A tragedy for those who feel! Yet according to numerous researchers, including Antonio Damasio (1994), Daniel Goleman (1994, 1998), and James Zull (2002), the emotions are intimately connected to thought, and may in fact run the show more than we realize. According to these researchers, the following are true:

1. Emotions reside in the brain making them truly brain-based.
2. There are observable neural connections between our emotions and our intellect.
3. Our emotions affect our ability to learn and to make decisions.
4. Emotions are not separate from learning and teaching but integral to them.

For the most part, teachers and administrators in this country have tended to disregard the importance of emotions in the classroom. But once it was established incontrovertibly that emotions were housed in the brain, those involved in education realized they had to give emotions a second look.

Below I offer three Emotional Principles associated with brain-based learning that I believe we, as teachers, should hold firmly in mind.

Emotional Principle #1

Our emotions and our intellect are intertwined.

Our emotional center, the limbic system, is located deep inside the brain, some might say in the "heart" of the brain (see Figure 8.1 on page 141). In order to more fully understand how our emotions are connected to our intellect, let's examine two central components of the limbic system—the hippocampus and the amygdala.

The hippocampus, like all structures in the limbic brain, is located in both the left and right hemispheres. Shaped like a seahorse, the hippocampus organizes factual information and sends it into our long-term memory. The hippocampus is extremely susceptible to the stress hormone cortisol. Although cortisol receptors are found throughout the brain, they are most prominent in the hippocampus. In fact, researchers have found that "stress in adults has been shown to regulate the number of cortisol receptors in the hippocampus" (Jacobs and Nadel, 1985, p. 518).

The hippocampus is linked with spatial behavior such as remembering where objects are located or reading a road map to navigate from one place to another. In essence, the hippocampus helps us find our way from home to work, and in general it helps us get around in the world. In their book *The Hippocampus as a Cognitive Map*, researchers John O'Keefe and

Figure 8.1 The Hippocampus and Amygdala

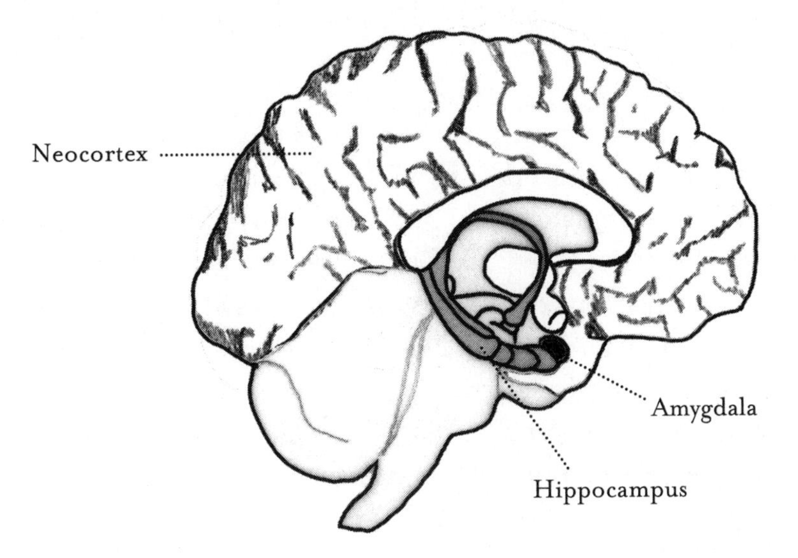

Lynn Nadel (1978) argues that the hippocampus also helps us navigate our brain, meaning that when we try to find where an obscure fact is stored (say, our childhood street address), the hippocampus will guide us to where it has been stored unused for years. Stress inhibits the hippocampus from performing its functions effectively.

The amygdala is an almond-shaped structure that permanently stores our most intense negative and positive emotions; it enables us to monitor and make meaning out of our experiences. The amygdala is constantly screening sensory input. It influences our ideas and ability to judge. In *The Emotional Brain*, Joseph LeDoux writes:

> The amygdala has a greater influence on the cortex than the cortex has on the amygdala, allowing emotional arousal to dominate and control thinking. . . . Although thoughts can easily trigger emotions (by activating the amygdala), we are not very effective at willfully turning off emotions (by deactivating the amygdala) (p. 301).

The extensive neural connections between the limbic system and the neocortex, indicate that feelings are a part of our thinking and learning.

LeDoux has discovered neural pathways that run between our limbic system and our neocortex (see Figure 8.1). Although we can see that the neural passageways flow both ways between our neocortex and our amygdala, it is important to note, as LeDoux has shown, that more neural connections run from the amygdala to our neocortex than vice versa. This means that our "emotional brain" can and will take control of our "thinking brain" when we least expect it. This phenomenon is called "downshifting."

Why Downshift?

In our early history, in order for humans to survive the very real physical threats that were part of the landscape, our ancestors needed a mechanism to assess and respond to potential danger, what is known as the fight-or-flight response. When our limbic system sends signals that the environment is not safe, a large amount of blood leaves the cortex and goes into the limbic brain and the brain stem, causing us either to flee, or if that isn't possible, to fight. When the majority of blood and oxygen shifts down to these lower centers of the brain, effective cognitive reasoning cannot take place. Today, even though we do not have to fight off wild animals, we can witness the same phenomenon of downshifting almost daily in our classrooms, lunchrooms, school buses, and playgrounds.

When a child feels angry or threatened, the blood and oxygen literally downshift from the neocortex (the "thinking cap") to the brain stem, the primitive reptilian brain. When this happens the child reacts physically instead of thinking through the situation. Downshifting leaves the child unable to think clearly.

In the classroom, when our students' amygdala perceives something as threatening, the information we're teaching simply does not make it into the cortex. Robert Sylwester (1995) explains that in the classroom, our emotions determine what we pay attention to, and what we pay attention to influences what we learn. A calmer limbic system means clearer thinking. If we apply these concepts to our teaching, it becomes clear that if we can engage our students' emotions in a positive manner, they will be more likely to focus on the content of our lessons.

Emotional Principle #2

The neural connections between our emotions and our intellect influence our ability to pay attention and to make decisions.

We've seen that our emotions and our intellect are connected. Indeed, our emotions help us filter sensory input (Feden and Vogel, 2003), which as you recall from Chapter Six, must be transferred to working memory within 30 seconds if we are to process it and link it to long-term memory.

In effect, our emotional system drives the decision of whether or not we pay attention to incoming stimuli. It tells us whether or not something is important and determines if a situation is safe. Let's say that you're hiking in the woods, and in your peripheral vision you see something brown and curved on the ground. Your first thought is "snake!" which your emotional system identifies as important and unsafe. Your amygdala gets the message first and sends you into a fight-or-flight mode. Your heart rate increases and you take action, jumping quickly away from the object. You look again and see that what you'd thought was a poisonous snake is only a large, twisted stick. Only after your neocortex can determine what the object truly is, do you calm down. In this situation, your intellect was not engaged; your limbic system took over based on emotional data and controlled your actions.

Only when these two conditions—importance and safety—are met will the emotional system allow the brain to pay attention to incoming input in a way that will facilitate academic learning (moving it to working memory where it can be connected to what is already known to create new knowledge).

Emotional Principle #3

Students benefit in a classroom environment that is perceived as safe, joyful, and challenging.

Our brains make a clear distinction between challenge, a "combination of personal interest or intrinsic motivation together with a sense of empowerment," and threat "a feeling of helplessness" or stress (Caine, Caine, and Crowell, 1994).

Our brain is affected when stress is sustained for months and years on end. Physiologically, during stressful times, our heart rate increases, and the stress hormone cortisol is secreted. Goleman says "cortisol steals energy resources from the working memory—from the intellect—and shunts them to the senses" (1999, p. 76). In the classroom, continual stress will have a negative effect on our students' ability to learn and think clearly, as threats and stress inhibits learning and the functioning of intelligence.

What can we do as teachers to alleviate stress in the classroom for our students? How do we work toward creating a classroom environment that is safe and joyful, yet challenging?

One effective approach is to teach our students about the brain. Students of all ages are fascinated to learn how they learn. Through graphics and explanations teachers can explain about the reptilian brain, the mammal brain, and the human brain, and we can incorporate "Who Am I?" units for our students on their multiple intelligences, left-, right-, or middle-brain preference, and their learning styles. I also recommend teaching an age-appropriate unit on how to maintain a healthy brain through keeping healthy physically by drinking water, exercising, and eating a balanced diet, as discussed in Chapter Three.

Teachers can also alleviate the stress many students feel by immediately starting to implement the following suggestions:

- Agree not to call on students unless they have their hand up.
- Vary the type of homework and class assignments so that all students will be able to work in their area(s) of strength at least part of the day.
- Model respect for the students. Tell them you are doing this and explain why respect is important in your classroom.
- Have a rule that we respect others at all times, in the classroom and in all school rooms.
- Do not allow bullying or any type of belittling in your classroom. (Rick Lavoie (2002b) reports that approximately 160,000 American children are absent on any given day due to fear of "intimidation or humiliation at the hands of their school mates.")
- Tell students it is okay to make mistakes. Explain to students that everyone makes mistakes, including yourself from time to time.
- Show them that making mistakes is part of the learning process.
- Portray a sense of optimism. (Consult Martin Seligman's *The Optimistic Child* and *Learned Optimism* for ideas.)
- Show confidence in your students' ability to succeed.
- Use a positive and enthusiastic tone of voice when you teach.

Lavoie discusses how he was advised to be stern and inflexible at the beginning of the school year, and "never smile until December." His response to that recommendation is "baloney!" Lavoie (2002a) recommends that we interact with our students in a warm and friendly manner each and every day. He says, "Smile! Laugh! Learn their names! Before they care how much you know, they gotta know how much you care!"

In the next section, we will examine Goleman's theory of emotional intelligence, a theory that is based on neurological research. We can use this theory both as a basis for assessing our own emotional intelligence, and as a way to reach our students using positive emotions. After all, we want our students' limbic brain to signal the message to their neocortex that it is safe to learn in our classroom.

Table 8.1 The Five Dimensions of Emotional Intelligence and their Connections to Multiple Intelligences

Goleman's Emotional Dimensions	Description	Connection to Intrapersonal and Interpersonal Intelligences
1. Self-Awareness	Knowing one's internal states, preferences, resources and intuitions	Intrapersonal
2. Self-Regulation	Managing one's internal states, impulses, and resources	Intrapersonal
3. Motivation	Emotional tendencies that guide or facilitate reaching goals	Intrapersonal
4. Empathy	Awareness of others' feelings, needs, and concerns	Interpersonal
5. Social Skills	Adeptness at inducing desirable responses in others	Interpersonal

Emotional Intelligence

Goleman is the originator of the concept "emotional intelligence." When it comes to the "head versus heart" argument I discussed at the beginning of this chapter, Goleman and his colleagues have more or less turned the tables: They believe that in most circumstances, emotional intelligence is at least as important as academic smarts, and sometimes, it's actually more valuable.

In *Emotional Intelligence* (1994) and *Working with Emotional Intelligence* (1998), Goleman cites numerous examples where people's "low emotional IQ" got in the way of their being hired or promoted. Emotional intelligence matters. For example, if two highly qualified applicants are applying for the same position, the one who is perceived as being the "best fit emotionally" is likely to be the one who gets the job. Many of us know people who are very smart, yet who do not understand how to get along with others. They do not know how to join a conversation or how to convey interest in others' lives. These people could be said to have a high academic IQ and a low emotional IQ, or what Goleman calls "EQ."

What constitutes emotional intelligence? Let's examine Goleman's five areas of emotional intelligence. In so doing, we can also overlap the two theories of emotional intelligence with two of the multiple intelligences.

Goleman's five areas of emotional intelligence are self-awareness, self-regulation, motivation, empathy, and social skills. A brief description of these areas is provided in Table 8.1. You will see that these five categories of emotional intelligence correspond to Gardner's interpersonal and intrapersonal intelligences.

Emotional Intelligence and Knowing Yourself

Goleman (1994) believes that "knowing yourself" is the most important aspect of emotional intelligence. I agree. In order to truly understand others, we have to know and understand ourselves first. The more we understand ourselves, the more we will be able to understand others. Our emotional intelligence gives us a sense of who we are and what we believe; from there we can get a solid sense of who our students are and what they believe.

Our Emotional Profile

Goleman (1998) believes that each of us has our own unique emotional intelligence profile. Take some time now to complete the Emotional Intelligence Questionnaire for Teachers on pages 147–148, and then write your results in the Emotional Intelligence Mirror.

After taking the emotional intelligence questionnaire, it might be beneficial to reflect on the results and, if appropriate, to set a goal to increase an area. In my own case, after taking the emotional intelligence questionnaire, I became aware of the following: Although I could speak effectively to my classes and at conferences, I was less comfortable speaking in small groups made up of my peers. I realized that this was a hindrance I wished to be free of. I therefore made a goal to "state my opinion at least once during small faculty meetings."

Emotional Intelligence in the Classroom

As was stated at the beginning of this chapter, by and large American teachers have not attended to the "emotional climate" of the classroom. The findings from Goleman's theory, however, give us "permission" to look at our students as emotional beings and they suggest ways to provide our students with an in-depth understanding of their emotional life.

Teachers can use the concept of emotional intelligence to help students understand their own feelings and to have empathy for others. LeDoux (1996) states, "Emotion and cognition are best thought of as separate but interacting mental functions mediated by separate but interacting brain systems" (p. 69). Neurologists have demonstrated that "neurons that fire together, wire together" and that "repeated firing of neuronal networks can

Emotional Intelligence Questionnaire for Teachers

Check each statement that describes you.

1. Self-Awareness

___✓___ I am aware of what I am feeling most of the time.

___✓___ I know that I have weaknesses; I am usually able to admit when I have made a mistake.

___✓___ I know that I have strengths; I am usually able to feel good with myself when I have accomplished a goal or completed a good deed.

___✓___ People would say that I have a "presence."

___✓___ I mentor my students.

2. Self- Regulation

___✓___ I am organized and careful in my work at school.

___✓___ I make new goals for myself and hold myself accountable for meeting them.

___✓___ Generally speaking, people trust me to do what I say I am going to do.

___✓___ I often come up with new solutions to solve problems.

___✓___ When conflicts arise at work, I rise to the occasion by staying calm and positive.

3. Motivation

___✓___ I work hard to prepare the best units and lessons for my students.

___✓___ I frequently implement promising new teaching strategies.

___✓___ I believe that I will be successful in most of my classroom endeavors.

___✓___ I actively support the initiatives, and the mission, of my school.

___✓___ I am constantly looking for ways to improve my teaching skills.

4. Empathy

___✓___ I strive to set up and maintain a classroom that encourages productivity and promotes positive emotional growth.

___✓___ I strive to understand how my students are feeling, and seek ways to ensure that they are comfortable taking academic risks in my classroom.

✓ I welcome diversity in my classroom—diversity of different cultures as well as students with special needs.

✓ I sense how the parents of my students feel at parent-teacher meetings.

✓ I work toward mentoring new teachers, or assisting other teachers in the building when I can.

5. Social Skills

_____ I frequently take a leadership position in the school by volunteering to serve on committees or sponsor after-school activities.

_____ I actively mediate when two colleagues are in disagreement.

_____ I cultivate supportive relationships with other teachers, specialists, and/or administrators in the school building.

_____ I listen to others' points of view, but make strong efforts to assert my point of view as well.

_____ I work hard to initiate a change at school when I see the need. For example, after learning about a new reading program that I feel will help our students, I will enlist the support of others to bring this program to our school.

Scoring—Tally and total the number of checks in each of Goleman's five domains.

_____ Self-Awareness

_____ Self-Regulation

_____ Motivation

_____ Empathy

_____ Social Skills

The strongest areas for you are those with 4–5 check marks.
The moderate areas for you are those with 3 check marks.
The underdeveloped areas for you are those with 1–2 check marks.

My Reflection Mirror for Emotional Intelligence

Final Summary of My Emotional Intelligence

Emotional Intelligence Areas	Results—Rate as Strong, Moderate, or Weak Areas
1. Self Awareness	
2. Self-Regulation	
3. Motivation	
4. Empathy	
5. Social Skills	

I find it interesting that I am so capable at . . .

Overall, one area that I want to improve in is . . .

I have a goal to ______________________________________

______________________________________ **at home**

and to ______________________________________

______________________________________ **at school.**

produce growth of new connections" (Zull, 2002, p. 223). It stands to reason that as teachers, we would want to teach our students about their emotions, so that they can come to understand, accept, and control their feelings.

Goleman believes that the cornerstone of emotional intelligence is self-awareness. Self-awareness means being smart about what we feel. When we're self-aware we're using our limbic system and our neocortex simultaneously, both feeling and thinking.

But how do we teach our students to do this? Teachers could point out to students different scenarios about how to recognize and control one's emotions. For example, suppose a student, Roger, gets into a fight with his father before school. He is upset on the school bus, and still upset when he walks into Mrs. McMillan's fourth-grade class. After being in school 10 minutes, he deliberately knocks over some desks and gets sent to the principal's office.

If we routinely teach our students about the brain, the emotions, and emotional intelligence, we can teach Roger to recognize what he is feeling (in this case anger) and to analyze this feeling. If Roger could see that he is angry only with his father, he could begin to plan how to deal with his father, and not carry this anger onto the school bus and into the school building. If we teach Roger about self-awareness, he can begin to develop successful coping mechanisms.

We can help students with anger issues to recognize their feelings. We can teach them to use their neocortex to think about what is bothering them when they are angry instead of lashing out against a classmate. Pat Wolfe is a neurologist interested in connecting neurological findings to the classroom. In her audiotape, *Translating Brain Research into Educational Practice* (1996), Wolfe describes a fourth-grade teacher who taught her students about the Triune Brain theory. The teacher explained that when we think, we are mostly using the neurons in our neocortex; this causes most of the blood and oxygen in the brain to remain in the neocortex. When we lash out in anger without thinking, it is a sign that a lot of the blood and oxygen have downshifted from our neocortex and into our limbic brain and brain stem, down to a fight-or-flight mentality. In Wolfe's audiotape there is a scene on the playground where the fourth-grade class is having recess. One boy is starting to pick a fight with another boy, and a girl yells, "Sam, get back into your neocortex! Don't downshift! Think!" Sure enough, Sam stops.

As we know, emotions tell our students if they should pay attention to the teacher, or daydream instead. Teachers can use Goleman's five dimensions as a framework to set up and maintain a safe and challenging classroom and to reflect on their own emotional strengths and weaknesses. There are myriad ways we can incorporate emotional intelligence into our lessons. Below I will discuss a few of these.

Literature-based discussion

Planned discussion that utilizes a reading of designated books constitutes one terrific way to teach about emotions. Librarian Judith Rovenger notes the wealth of experience that books have to offer:

> *Sharing stories and books is an important part of helping children understand themselves, other people, and the world in which they live. . . . By reading about others who have also experienced fear of the dark, sadness over the loss of a toy, anger at a sibling, embarrassment at being teased, or distress over being bullied, children realize they are not abnormal or weird or alone. By identifying with characters in a book, they can learn to accept themselves* (2000, p. 40).

We can use books to illustrate each of Goleman's five areas of emotional intelligence. Table 8.2 provides a list of books for each area as recommended by Rovenger.

Movie and television viewing

Video use is a technique similar to literature-based discussion, except that here, we use movies and television to explore areas that are emotionally affecting. Our students can benefit from watching selected television dramas or comedies followed by guided discussion.

For example, let's say you and your class have just watched the movie *Going to the Mat.* This is a drama about a boy named Andrew, who is blind. When Andrew moves from New York to Utah he has difficulty being accepted by his classmates. Andrew takes up wrestling in the hopes of gaining acceptance. After viewing, students can discuss various issues raised in the story through large-group or small-group discussion. The interpersonal, intrapersonal, and existential intelligences are all involved here. You can incorporate drawing, collage, and music to enliven other intelligences as well.

Role-playing

Role-playing is an excellent way to incorporate empathy into our lessons. Students can role-play scenes from literature books or historical events. When students role-play, they can create and perform skits that help them

Table 8.2 Emotional Intelligence and Recommended Books

Area of Emotional Intelligence	Recommended Books
1. Self-Awareness	• *Today I Feel Silly and Other Moods That Make My Day* by Jamie Lee Curtis • *No Good in Art* by Miram Cohen • *I Never Win!* by Judy Delton
2. Self-Regulation	• *Alexander, Who Used to Be Rich Last Sunday* by Judith Viorst • *I Can Do It By Myself* by Lessie Little • *Tales of a Fourth Grade Nothing* by Judy Blume
3. Motivation	• *Ramona Quimby, Age 8* by Beverly Cleary • *Muggie Maggie* by Beverly Cleary • *The Little Engine that Could* by Watty Piper
4. Empathy	• *Guess Who My Favorite Person Is* by Byrd Baylor • *Jafta's Mother* by Hugh Lewin • *The Other Emily* by Gibbs Davis.
5. Social Skills	• *Better With Two* by Barbara Joose • *Sometimes It's O.K. to Be Angry* by Mitch Golant

feel what another character is feeling. Gloria Wilson is an educator who frequently uses role-playing in her lessons. She notes that acting helps students express their emotions and articulate their thoughts (2004). In other words, let's suppose you have a student named Sally who gets angry too easily. If she is assigned to role-play a character who tries to understand someone's point of view before overreacting, Sally gets to experience an alternative way to behave.

You might try role-playing after the discussion that follows a book or movie viewing. For example, after watching *Going to the Mat* several students could role-play Andrew and his classmates. They might be able to "feel" the other students' reactions. Role-plays can include dance, costumes, homemade props, and music, appealing to a broad range of students' multiple intelligences.

Planned Sharing

Planned sharing is a method teachers can use to enhance student-teacher interaction. Simply put, planned sharing is a positive, happy emotional intervention in which teachers think of different ways to share their lives with their students. One second-grade teacher told me that her students were surprised and thrilled to find out that she had a cocker spaniel. She brought in pictures of Cookie, and described to her class some of the mischief they encountered together. She told me that when some of these students were third- and fourth-graders, they still stopped her in the hallways to ask about Cookie.

Other things that teachers can share are funny episodes and pictures of their spouse and children, or their parents. One fifth-grade teacher told me that she brings her guitar to school sometimes and plays songs for the class. One day she distributed the lyrics to a song and asked the students to discuss the meaning of it. You could take this one step further and turn it into a writing assignment.

Why is this sharing beneficial? It lets students see an appropriate personal side of us that may enable them to feel more comfortable with us as a person, and as their teacher as well. Of course, planned sharing also includes time for teachers to get to know students on appropriate personal levels. We can learn about their pets, hobbies, sports, after-school activities, hikes, Girl Scout and Boy Scout events, and musical endeavors.

An Emotional Intelligence Lesson

In addition to the activities above, you can teach lessons that help students develop their emotional intelligence. The following lesson, adapted from *Connecting with Others: Lessons for Teaching Social and Emotional Competence, Grades 3-5* (Coombs-Richardson, 2004), helps students discover how to express themselves in positive, constructive ways.

Topic: Communication: Understanding assertive, nonassertive, and aggressive behaviors (can be integrated with language arts or health unit)

Objectives: To understand that people choose how they respond to a situation; to learn assertive communication strategies

Introduce the topic and objectives; provide the following definitions to the students:

1. *Assertive behavior:* Assertive behavior is expressing feelings and thoughts in a direct and honest way. When you behave in an assertive manner, you make yourself and others feel good. Acting assertively is a way to show respect, both for your self and for others.
2. *Nonassertive behavior:* Nonassertive behavior is not telling your feelings or thoughts. When you behave in a nonassertive way, you hurt yourself because you often do not get what you want.
3. *Aggressive behavior:* Aggressive behavior is expressing feelings and thoughts in ways that belittle or overpower others. When you behave in an aggressive way, you hurt others, because you are not taking their feelings into consideration.

Students choose two of the following activities to explore these concepts:

1. Use puppets to play scenes where two or more characters are involved in a potentially uncomfortable situation.
2. Role-play a scenario at the school water fountain. Roger and Matt both claim that they are next in line and therefore next to get his drink. Pairs act out this scene, taking turns being aggressive, nonassertive, and assertive.
3. Use clay to illustrate their perceptions of the three concepts.
4. Read the first part of a story, the part that sets up the problem. Students create different assertive, nonassertive, and assertive ways to solve the problem.
5. Watch an age-appropriate television show with the goal to find characters exhibiting each of the three behaviors. Students pause the recording at scenes in which a character demonstrates assertive, nonassertive, or aggressive behavior and discuss. This could be pretaped and watched in class, or assigned as homework. At the end of the show, students write up what they noticed about the different types of behavior.
6. Study and discuss a comic strip that demonstrates aggressive, nonassertive, or assertive behaviors. (The Sunday comics are an excellent resource for this activity.)
7. Make a list of things that they get angry about, and then write a constructive solution on what can be done about the anger in each situation.

At the end of the lesson, students share what they have done and discuss the assertive strategies they have developed.

Other books that are filled with activities and instructions on how to use emotional intelligence in the classroom include: *50 Activities for*

Teaching Emotional Intelligence, Level 1: Elementary by Dianne Schilling and Susanna Palomares, and *Fostering Emotional Intelligence in K-8 Students* by Gwen Doty.

If our students feel more comfortable with us, if they can trust us, brain-based learning research shows that they are more likely to strive harder to make academic gains. They know that they can trust us to respect them and take their efforts seriously. If we introduce some of the activities described above, along with open discussion, reflective individual assignments, and stimulating group activities, we will be well on our way to strengthening our students' emotional intelligence.

As I've tried to make clear throughout this chapter, the more we tune into the emotions of our students, the more they will be able to learn in, and out, of the classroom. Tuning into our emotions and the emotions of our students will help all of us feel safe and enlivened in our teaching environments.

Afterword

"Teaching and learning is a lifelong process, not an event, or a class, or a day at school. One does not just simply become a great teacher; one simply commits to it as a path."

—Eric Jensen (1995, p. 72)

Teaching is all about making connections. In this book, we have examined many brain-based teaching and learning strategies that foster connections, including creating safe home and school environments, connecting new knowledge to prior knowledge, and allowing time for practice and reflection to strengthen neural pathways and create superhighways. As you can see, teachers are in a unique position to serve as connectors—connecting to students on a personal level and helping students connect to academic content and develop the neural connections in their brains.

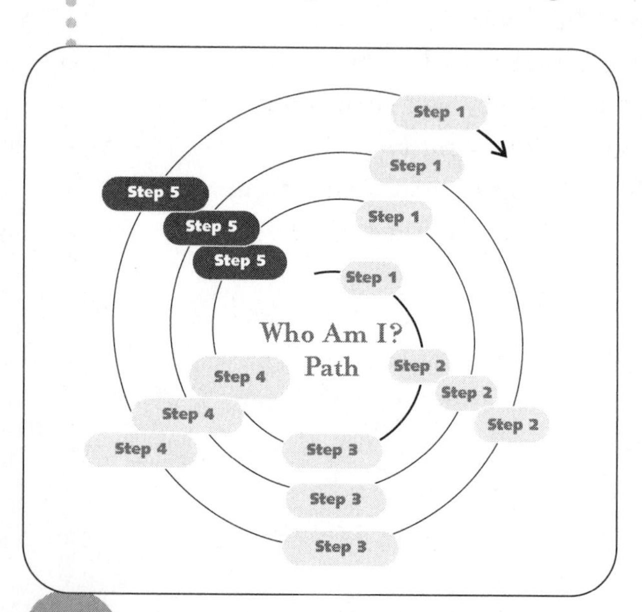

Pulling It All Together—One Last Look at the Spiral Path

In the first step on the spiral path, we learned about the brain. We gained an in-depth understanding of neural connections from cognitive and affective perspectives. We also learned about the principles of brain-based learning and the effects of healthy home and classroom environments on the brain.

In the second step along the spiral path, we increased our self-awareness. We learned that each of us embodies a unique combination of cognitive and affective traits, including our own neural connections, our left-/right-/middle-brain preference, our multiple intelligences, our information-processing-based learning style, and our emotional intelligence. The questionnaires and observations of our teaching patterns helped us examine our neurologically based strengths and weaknesses. The student questionnaires allowed us to discover the strengths and preferences of our students, which we learned can influence our teaching choices.

Step three was analytical. We asked, "How do I currently teach using my current neurological profile?" We analyzed our teaching methods using cognitive and affective lenses. We discovered that we tend to teach using our neurological strengths. However, this primarily allows us to reach students with learning styles similar to ours.

Spiraling to step four, we were asked to teach using more of our moderately developed and underdeveloped areas. We were asked to design and teach lessons in ways that were relatively unfamiliar. We used our weaknesses to reach the strengths of some of our students.

This fourth step is an important one. I am hoping that by becoming aware of your less-developed hemisphere, and your less-developed intelligences, you will start to use these more often in the classroom. Combining your less-used teaching techniques, along with your more frequently used teaching techniques, should enable you to reach your students in their strongest areas. Your students will be thrilled to have some of their classroom and homework assignments fall within their area(s) of strength. Completing assignments in this way promotes enthusiasm, success, and hope in the mind's eye of our students. Our students will also benefit as they complete the "Who Am I?" exercises for students. Their self-awareness and confidence will increase as they realize that they can have choice and control in the direction of their lives.

The fifth step is really a continuation step. It is symbolic of the fact that our brains, and the brains of our students, are always growing and changing. We continue to read professional literature, keep up with current developments in brain research, and apply our new knowledge in the classroom. In effect, our brain-based learning spiral path continues forever as we learn new information and expand our teaching repertoire.

In this hectic day and age, I hope that this book has provided you with time to learn more about yourself. I hope that you feel renewed, refreshed, inspired, and validated. I hope that you have enjoyed reflecting upon "Who You Are" from the different brain-based learning avenues, and that you have come to see yourself in a new light. Finally, I hope that you have found new brain-based-learning teaching and strategies that you will enjoy using with your students.

As teachers, we connect with our students from early September through June via intensive academic and emotional avenues. It is my hope that you, and the students you teach, are connected, and that you will all have joyful and meaningful school experiences now, and in the years ahead.

Bibliography

Armstrong, T. (1994). *Multiple intelligences in the classroom.* Alexandria, VA: Association for Supervision and Curriculum Development.

Armstrong, T. (2000). *Multiple intelligences in the classroom* (2nd ed.) Alexandria, VA: Association for Supervision and Curriculum Development.

Armstrong, T. (1993). *Seven kinds of smart.* New York: Plume.

Armstrong, T. (2003). *You're smarter than you think: A kid's guide to multiple intelligences.* Minneapolis, MN: Free Spirit Pub.

Caine, G., Caine, R., & Crowell, S. (1994). *Making connections: Teaching and the human brain.* Menlo Park, CA: Addison-Wesley.

Caine, G., Caine, R., & Crowell, S. (1999). *MindShifts* (2nd ed.) Tucson, AZ: Zephyr Press.

Campbell, B. (1989). Multiplying intelligence in the classroom. *New Horizons for Learning, IX (2)*, 7.

Campbell, L., Campbell, B., & Dickinson, D. (1996). *Teaching and learning through multiple intelligences.* Needham Heights, MA: Allyn & Bacon.

Cherry, C., Godwin, D., & Staples, J. (1989). *Is the left brain always right?* Carthage, IL: Fearon.

Connell, D. (2002, September). Left brain/right brain. *Instructor*, 28-32, 89.

Connell, D. (2000). Brain-based teaching—integrating multiple intelligences and emotional intelligence. *Classroom Leadership*, 4 (3), 4-7.

Connell, D., & Gunzelman, B. (2004, March). The new gender gap. *Instructor*, 14-18.

Coombs-Richardson, R. (2004). *Connecting with Others: Lessons for Teaching Social and Emotional Competence, Grades 3-5.* Champaign, IL: Research Press.

Crane, L. (1989). *Alert scale of cognitive style.* Kalamazoo, MI: Department of Communication, Western Michigan University.

Damasio, A. (1994). *Descarte's error: Emotion, reason, and the human brain.* New York: Grosset/Putnam.

D'Arcangelo, M. (1998). The brains behind the brain. *Educational Leadership, 56 (3)*, 20-25.

Diamond, M. (1998). *Magic trees of the mind.* New York: Dutton.

Doty, G. (2001). *Fostering emotional intelligence in K–8 students.* Thousand Oaks, CA: Corwin Press.

Dryfoos, J. (2000). The mind-body-building equation. *Educational Leadership, 57 (6)*, 14-17.

Feden, P., & Vogel, R. (2003). *Methods of teaching—applying cognitive science to promote student learning.* Boston, MA: McGraw Hill.

Frender, G. (1990). *Learning to learn.* Nashville, TN: Incentive Publications, Inc.

Frender, G. (1994). *Teaching for learning success.* Nashville, TN: Incentive Publications.

Gardner, H. (1983). *Frames of mind: The theory of multiple intelligences.* New York: Basic Books.

Gardner, H. (1993). *Multiple intelligences: The theory in practice.* New York: Basic Books.

Gardner, H. (1998, April 23). Keynote presentation, New York: Fourth International Teaching for Intelligence Conference.

Gardner, H. (1999). *Intelligence reframed: Multiple intelligences for the 21st century.* New York: Basic Books.

Goldstein, E. B. (2005). *Cognitive psychology: Connecting minds, research, and everyday experience.* Belmont, CA: Wadsworth.

Goleman, D. (1994). *Emotional intelligence—why it can matter more than IQ.* New York: Bantam.

Goleman, D. (1998). *Working with emotional intelligence.* New York: Bantam.

Hannaford, C. (1995). *Smart moves—why learning is not all in your head.* Arlington, VA: Great Ocean Publishers.

Hardiman, M. (2003). *Connecting brain research with effective teaching.* Lanham, MD: The Scarecrow Press.

Izard, C. E. (1992). Basic emotions, relations among emotions, and emotion-cognition relations. *Psychological Review, 99*, 561-565.

Jacobs, W. J., & Nadel, L. (1985). Stress-induced recovery of fears and phobias. *Psychological Review, 92 (4)*, 512-531.

Jensen, E. (1996). *Brain-based learning.* Del Mar, CA: Turning Point Publishing.

Jensen, E. (2000). *Brain-based learning—the new science of teaching and training.* San Diego, CA: The Brain Store.

Jensen, E. (1995). *Super teaching.* San Diego, CA: The Brain Store.

Kephart, N. (1971). *The slow learner in the classroom.* Columbus, OH: Merrill Publishing.

Kolb, B., & Whishaw, I. (2000). *Fundamentals of human neuropsychology* (4th ed.). University of Lethbridge, W.H. Freeman and Company, Worth Publishers.

Kotulak, R. (1997) *Inside the brain—revolutionary discoveries of how the mind works.* Kansas City, MO: Andrews McMeel Publishing.

Lavoie, R. (2002). Tales from the road. Teacher tip of the month. (September). www.ldonline.org.

Lavoie, R. (2002). Teacher tip of the month. (October). www.ldonline.org.

Lambert, L. (2000). The new physical education. *Educational Leadership, 57(6)*, 34-38.

Lawry, J. (2003). Multiple intelligences, Howard Gardner and new methods in college teaching. *Caritas in the classroom: Strategies for unearthing the genius in our students.* Jersey City, NJ: New Jersey City University Publishing.

LeDoux, J. (1996). *The emotional brain—the mysterious underpinnings of emotional life.* New York: Touchstone.

LeDoux, J. (2002). *Synaptic self: how our brains become who we are.* New York: Viking.

Lerner, J. (1993). *Learning disabilities—theories, diagnosis, and teaching strategies* (6th ed.). New York: Houghton Mifflin.

London, W. (1988). Brain/mind bulletin collections. *New Science Bulletin. 13*, 7c.

Maslow, A. (1970). A theory of human motivation. *Motivation and personality* (2nd ed.) New York: Harper & Row Publishers

Matthews, G. B. (1996). *The philosophy of childhood.* Cambridge, MA: Harvard University Press.

MacLean, P. D. (1969). New trends in man's evolution. In *A Triune Concept of the Brain and Behavior.* [Papers presented at Queen's University, Ontario, 1969.] Ann Arbor, MI: Books on Demand, University Microfilms International.

MacLean, P. D. (1978). A mind of three minds: Educating the triune brain. In J. Chall & A. Mirsky (eds.), *Education and the Brain.* Chicago: Chicago University Press.

Meyer, M. (1997). The greening of learning: Using the eighth intelligence. *Educational Leadership, 55 (1)*, 32-34.

Nelson, K. N. (1998). *Developing students' multiple intelligences.* New York: Scholastic.

O'Keefe, J., & Nadel L. (1978). *The Hippocampus as a cognitive map.* New York: Claredon Press.

Pollack, W. (1998). *Real boys.* New York: Henry Holt.

Pollack, W. (2000). *Real boys' voices.* New York: Penguin.

Ramey, C., & Ramey, S. (1996). *Prevention of intellectual disabilities: Early interventions to improve cognitive development.* Birmingham, AL: University of Alabama Civitan International Research Center.

Restak, R. (2001). *Mozart's brain and the fighter pilot.* New York: Harmony Books.

Richardson, R. (1996). *Connecting with others: Lessons for teaching social and emotional competence.* Chicago, IL: Research Press.

Rovenger, J. (2000). Fostering emotional intelligence. *School Library Journal, 46 (12)*, 40-41.

Scherer, M. (1997). Perspectives: Martian chronicles. *Educational Leadership, 55 (1)*, 7.

Seligman, M. (1998). *Learned optimism: How to change your mind and your life.* New York: Simon & Schuster.

Seligman, M. (1996). *The optimistic child: Proven program to safeguard children from depression and build life-long resistance.* New York: HarperTrade.

Semrud, M., & Hynd G.W. (1990). Right hemispheric dysfunction in nonverbal learning disabilities: Social, academic, and adaptive functioning in adults and children. *Psychological Bulletin,* 107, 196–209.

Schilling, D. & Palomares, D. (1996). *50 activities for teaching emotional intelligence: Level 1, grades 1-5 elementary school.* Carson, CA: Innerchoice.

Smith, C. R. (1998). *Learning disabilities—the interaction of learner, task, and setting* (4th ed.). Boston: Allyn and Bacon.

Smith, K., & Gouze, K. (2004). *The sensory sensitive child.* New York: Harper Collins.

Springer, S., & Deutsch, G. (1998). Left brain, right brain: Perspectives from cognitive neuroscience (5th ed). New York: Freeman and Co.

Stock Kranowitz, C. (2003). *The out-of-sync child: Recognizing and coping with sensory integration dysfunction.* New York: Skylight Press.

Sylwester, R. (1995). *A Celebration of neurons: An educator's guide to the human brain.* Alexandria, VA: Association for Supervision and Curriculum Development.

Thompson, S. (1997). *The source for nonverbal learning disorders.* East Moline, IL: Lingui Systems, Inc.

Wilson, G. (2004). Using videotherapy to access curriculum and enhance growth. *Teaching Exceptional Children, 36 (6)*, 32-37.

Wolfe, P. (2001). *Brain matters—translating research into classroom practice.* Alexandria, VA: ASCD.

Wolfe, P. (1996). *Translating brain research into educational practice.* [Live Satellite Broadcasts, #297154] Alexandria, VA: Association for Supervision and Curriculum Development.

Zajonic, R. (1980). Feeling and thinking: Preferences need no inferences. *American Psychologist, 35*, 151-175.

Zull, J. (2002). *The art of changing the brain—enriching the practice of teaching by exploring the biology of learning.* Sterling, VA: Stylus Publishing.

Children's Literature

Baylor, B. (1977). *Guess who my favorite person is.* New York: Scribner.

Blume, J. (2003). *Otherwise known as Sheila the great.* New York: Puffin.

Blume, J. (2003). *Tales of a fourth grade nothing.* New York: Puffin.

Bryan, D. (2001). *Honey from my heart for you, friend.* Nashville, TN: J. Countryman.

Cohen, M. (1980). *No good in art.* New York: Greenwillow.

Curtis, J. (1998). *Today I feel silly and other moods that make my day.* New York: Joanna Colter.

Cleary, B. (1990). *Muggie Maggie.* New York: HarperTrophy.

Cleary, B. (1981). *Ramona Quimby, age 8.* New York: HarperCollins.

Curtis, J. (1998). *Today I feel silly and other moods that make my day.* New York: Joanna Colter.

Davis, G. (1990). *The other Emily.* Boston: Houghton Mifflin.

Delton, J. (1991). *I never win!* Minneapolis, MN: Carolrhoda.

George, J. C. (1997). *There's an owl in the shower.* New York: HarperTrophy.

Golant, M. (1988). *Sometimes it's O.K. to be angry.* London: Tor Books.

Hansberry, L. (2002). *A raisin in the sun.* New York: Spark.

Joose, B. (1988). *Better with two.* New York: HarperCollins.

Lewin, H. (1983). *Jafta's mother.* Minneapolis, MN: Carolrhoda.

Little, L. (1978). *I can do it by myself.* New York: HarperCollins.

Mayer, M. (1992). *There's a nightmare in my closet.* New York: Puffin.

O'Connor. (1990). *I can be me.* King of Prussia, PA: Childswork/Childsplay.

Perkins, L. (2001). *All alone in the universe.* New York: HarperTrophy.

Piper, W. (1978). *The little engine that could.* New York: Grosset and Dunlap.

Polacco, P. (1993). *The bee tree.* New York: The Putnam & Grosset Group.

Polacco, P. (1992). *Mrs. Katz and Tush.* New York: Bantam Doubleday Dell.

Polacco, P. (1990). *Thundercake.* New York: The Putnam & Grosset Group.

Stockton, S. (2004). *The bee man of orn and other fanciful tales.* Holicong, PA: Wildside.

Viorst, J. (1987). *Alexander, who used to be rich last Sunday.* New York: Aladdin.

Zeman, L. (1999). *Gilgamesh the king.* Toronto: Tundra Books.

Zeman, L. (1998). *The last quest of Gilgamesh.* Toronto: Tundra Books.

Zeman, L. (1998). *The revenge of Ishtar.* Toronto: Tundra Books.

Web sites

Brain Gym
www.braingym.com
This Web site contains an in-depth explanation of Brain Gym and educational kinesiology. It also has information on books, videos, and tapes about Brain Gym.

Brain Connection: The Link to Learning
www.brainconnection.com
This is a Web resource sponsored by Scientific Learning. It offers a free monthly newsletter.

The LDA GRAM
www.ldaca.org
This Web site contains a multitude of articles and newsletter reports pertaining to learning disabilities and attention deficit hyperactivity disorder. There are links to other related Web sites, and a bookstore with hundreds of books on learning disabilities.

LD On Line
www.ldonline.org
This Web site features a free newsletter and a section titled "Ask the Experts" who include Rick Lavoie, Larry Silver, and Matthew Cohen. It also includes many articles on learning disabilities.